Tell Someone

Tell
Someone

YOU CAN SHARE
THE GOOD NEWS

GREG LAURIE

B&H
PUBLISHING GROUP
NASHVILLE, TENNESSEE

978-1-4336-9014-3

Published by B&H Publishing Group
Nashville, Tennessee

Dewey Decimal Classification: 248.5
Subject Heading: WITNESSING \ EVANGELISTIC WORK \
CHRISTIAN LIFE

2 3 4 5 6 7 8 • 20 19 18 17 16

This book is not written to make you feel bad or condemn you if you have not engaged others with the gospel message. This book is written to encourage and inspire you.

I want to share some stories from my own life of both failure and success in my attempts to share my faith. But the most important things you will find in this book are biblical principles that you can apply in your life. I have put these principles to the test over forty years of ministry in both one-on-one occasions and large-scale evangelistic events in arenas and stadiums.

If you will take the time to read this book from beginning to end, I believe that as you apply these biblical truths, you will be able to not only share your faith, but also bring others to Christ.

Contents

Introduction

In some ways, I was not meant to be.

You see, I was conceived out of wedlock. I was not planned by my beautiful, hard-partying mother, as she met up with some man in Long Beach, California. They had an alcohol-fueled night of passion together and never really had a relationship beyond that. When my mother found out she was pregnant, she quickly married another man she was involved with at the time, and his name was listed on my birth certificate as my biological father.

But here's the good news, for me at least: though not planned by my mother, my life was indeed planned by God, just as yours was. So, you see, I *was* meant to be!

This was just one in a string of one-night stands and failed marriages that littered my mother's life . . . and mine. Most of the guys my mom was attracted to were similar: barfly types. Usually he had one too many shirt buttons undone, was fast-talking and loose-living. When it was all said and done, she married and divorced seven times, with a lot of guys in between.

But inexplicably, one of the men my mother married was different from all the rest. His name was even different: Oscar Felix

Laurie. He did not hang out in bars, like the other men my mom was attracted to, but worked for the Bar Association as an attorney. He was a voracious reader, educated, hardworking, and did not even drink or smoke. I don't know what my mom saw in him!

Oscar was known for his honesty and personal integrity. He was a well-respected attorney practicing on the East Coast and was well on his way to a judgeship. Oscar did not just marry my mother. He also adopted me and was the only man in my tumultuous childhood who ever treated me as a father should treat a son.

Out of the blue, my mom left him one day. She picked me up at school in New Jersey and we drove to the airport. Destination: Honolulu, Hawaii. I was excited to be going to Hawaii for the first time, and I asked, "Where's Dad?"

"He's not coming," she coldly responded. And that was the end of her marriage to Oscar. There, waiting at the airport in Honolulu, was the next man my mother would marry. I would not see Oscar for the rest of my childhood. I was a broken-hearted little boy.

Something snapped in me after that and I became very cynical and closed off. This new man my mom married owned a bar on Waikiki Beach and was the meanest drunk I have ever seen. He almost killed my mother one night in an alcoholic haze, hitting her on the head with, as I recall, a wooden Don Quixote statue.

Fast-forward ten tumultuous years to the day my life changed for time and eternity.

Though only seventeen years old, I felt like I was already seventy. In addition to living with my mom for all of her escapades, I had made a string of bad decisions in my teen years that made my already troubled life worse. I had become fed up with the way I was living. I was searching for truth and purpose—and the very meaning of life itself. For me, finding that truth was a process of elimination.

Clearly, it was not to be found in the adult world I was exposed to. From my mother, I learned that alcohol did not solve any problems. In fact, it created new ones. I quickly became disillusioned with the drugs I used in my pursuit of some kind of inner peace, so I knew the answer wasn't there either.

Enter the Jesus Freaks

There was a group of outspoken Christians on our campus that we laughingly called "the Jesus freaks." They would talk about God as though He were their next-door neighbor and would carry Bibles wherever they went. I openly mocked them, but secretly respected them.

My friends warned me to steer clear of them, lest I end up converted. I laughed at such a suggestion, saying, "The last thing I would ever be is a Christian!"

Famous last words.

One day, out of sheer curiosity, I decided to check them out a little more closely. I should mention there was a girl involved too. She was talking between classes with someone I knew. Though she was not a beauty queen by any stretch, there was something about this mystery girl that drew me in. She had something I did not see in the other girls—a wholesomeness.

I walked up to her and my friend, who were chatting, and then I saw—tucked under her arm with a couple of textbooks—a Bible! I thought to myself, *What a complete waste of a cute girl! Why would anyone carry a Bible openly?* But I have to admit, I was intrigued. Sure, there were other pretty girls on campus, but for some reason, I could not suppress my curiosity about this particular one.

One day at lunchtime, I decided I would track her down and find out more about what she believed. I found her on the front lawn of our high school, sitting with her Christian friends for a Bible study. I was close enough to eavesdrop on what they were saying, but not so close that others would think I was joining their ranks. That, of course, would have been social suicide.

As I looked around at their smiling faces, I felt pity for them. *Why can't they be cynical, angry, and mad at the world—like me?* I wondered. But watching them as they sang songs about Jesus Christ, I had to admit they did seem happy. There were even a couple of them that used to be buddies of mine in elementary school who had their lives clearly changed for the better.

Then I tried a thought on for the first time: *What if the Christians are right? What if God can be known in a personal way?* I quickly dismissed these crazy thoughts, but I came back to them again. *What if?*

For the most part, I don't remember what the speaker said that day, except for one statement that hit my heart like a lightning bolt from Heaven. His statement was, "Jesus said, 'You are either for Me or against Me!'" I looked around at the Christians and thought, *They are surely for Him.* And since I was not one of them, I wondered, *Am I against Jesus Christ?*

Mind you, I always believed Jesus was out there somewhere. After all, Jesus was my "God of choice" when catastrophe hit. I would call out to Him when trouble struck, not sure if He was listening. I had seen all His movies, and liked them!

As a child, living with my grandparents while my mom was living her partying lifestyle, I would be taken to the church they attended on Sundays. None of what I heard there really connected with me, and I would draw cartoons on the church bulletin while the preacher droned on. My grandmother had a picture of Jesus hanging on the wall of her house that I would often stare at. I would think to myself, *It would be nice to know Him!* between bites of cereal and *Felix the Cat* cartoons on TV. But it had never occurred to me that I could know Him in a personal way until that day on my high school campus.

And that was the day I put my faith in Jesus Christ.

Back to the Future

Fast-forward again. Ten years later, I am the pastor of a church that we planted in Riverside, California, and it is having explosive growth. I've married a godly and beautiful young girl named Cathe. I had met her at a Bible study and we now had one son, Christopher. Being a parent was a new experience for me, and I only had one point of reference to think of in that regard: Oscar Laurie.

I started thinking about how I would like to see him again. I owed him a debt of gratitude. Most of all, I wanted to tell him about my faith in Jesus Christ. So I tracked him down in New Jersey, where he had always lived. He was no longer practicing law; he was retired now, and remarried.

After a short phone conversation, Oscar was eager to reconnect and he asked me to come visit him in his hometown and meet his new family. When Cathe, Christopher, and I disembarked from the train that carried us from New York City to New Jersey, he was there waiting for us.

Though it was the first time I had seen my dad in years, it was as though we picked up where we last left off. We spent hours talking about what happened in the time since we last saw each other. I discovered that he had tried to get custody of me, but my mom, even though she had no time for me, fought him tooth and nail.

That evening, his wife, Barbara, cooked us a delicious Italian meal and she asked me to tell her how I had become a Christian and a pastor. As I told my story, Barbara was very responsive, asking questions and really engaging. In sharp contrast, my father— Oscar Laurie, the attorney—sat at the other end of the table, hands pressed together in front of his face, listening intently to every word, but not showing any visible reaction. I felt as though the judge was listening to my testimony in a court of law and I was not doing very well!

After I finished telling my story, Barbara thanked and hugged me. My dad said he would see me in the morning.

As it turns out, my dad had recently had a heart attack; he had blacked out and lost control of his car, crashing into a pole. He could have easily died. He was now on a very strict diet and exercise regimen under his doctor's supervision. He had certain medications he had to take each day as well. Part of his daily routine was a morning walk, and he asked me to join him the next day.

He knocked on the door of my room at 6:00 a.m. the next morning. I was in a deep sleep, as it was 3:00 a.m. in my West Coast body. I was still rubbing the sleep out of my eyes as we stepped out of the house into the brisk New Jersey morning. Oscar said, "Greg, I was listening very carefully to everything you said last night about Jesus Christ."

"Oh good," I mumbled. Then he dropped the bombshell: "Greg, I would like to commit my life to follow Jesus Christ right now!" I could hardly believe my ears, for I did not think that what I had said the night before had any impact on him whatsoever. I had not planned on or expected such a response to the gospel.

"Dad," I said, "Let me go over it one more time." He patiently listened as I explained who Jesus was, why He came, and how a person could come into a personal relationship with Him. Again, my father said that he wanted to do exactly that.

"Well, Dad, you can pray right now and ask Jesus into your life, if you like." To my surprise, my father—respected attorney and heart attack survivor—dropped to his knees and said, "I'm ready, Greg." I had not planned on kneeling for this prayer, but since he was already down, I joined him on the dew-covered grass of the park we were walking through. We prayed, and Oscar Felix Laurie had his eternal address changed that day.

His life changed too, dramatically and quickly. Living and pastoring in California, I could not expect him to attend our church, so I found some promising prospects from the phone book (this was before the Internet). I made some phone calls, and sent my dad to a good Bible-teaching church. I returned a month later to check on his spiritual progress and he had already read the entire Bible! He was actively involved in his church and was blossoming spiritually in every way. It was one of the most amazing conversions I have ever seen.

He became a leader in his church and worked with the Gideons, distributing Bibles. His wife, Barbara, also committed her life to Christ and served in Chuck Colson's prison ministry. God graciously gave my dad fifteen more years of life, and now he is in Heaven.

This is what every follower of Jesus should be engaged in on a regular basis: sharing our faith, leading others to Christ, discipling them, and helping them to get grounded in the church—and then going out and doing it all again.

CHAPTER 1

Something Christians and Non-Christians Have in Common

Jesus said, "All authority has been given to Me in Heaven and on earth. Go therefore and make disciples of all the nations, baptizing them in the name of the Father and of the Son and of the Holy Spirit, teaching them to observe all things that I have commanded you; and lo, I am with you always, even to the end of the age" (Matt. 28:18–20). In Mark's Gospel, Jesus said, "Go into all the world and preach the Good News to everyone" (Mark 16:15 NLT).

This is the command from Jesus Himself, often referred to as the Great Commission. Yet, whenever you bring up the topic of evangelism, people often cringe.

It's been said, "There is one thing that believers and nonbelievers have in common: they are both uptight about evangelism," and that is true. When it comes to sharing the gospel, it seems we plan for failure far more often than success.

Maybe that's why statistics indicate that 95 percent of all Christians have never led another person to Christ. For many followers of Jesus, the Great Commission has instead become the Great *Omission*, and that is more than a pity; it's a travesty.

A Sin Not to Share

Let me state something that may shock you, but I believe it is true with all of my heart. To not share your faith, to not tell others about Jesus Christ, can be an actual sin.

When we think of sin, we envision breaking commandments and doing wrong things—and indeed that is sinful. But the Bible speaks of both sins of commission and sins of omission. A sin of commission is doing what you should not do. In contrast, a sin of omission is not doing what you should do. The Bible says, "To him who knows to do good and does not do it, to him it is sin" (James 4:17).

Let's say you were walking down the street and you heard people screaming. You looked in their direction and saw a house in flames. Someone then cried out, "There is a person in that building!" Let me ask you, if you were to keep walking without a passing thought to those in serious danger, would that be wrong? I would hope you would at the very least call 9-1-1. Even more, you might go into that building and try to rescue that person inside. To do nothing would be outright criminal.

Yet, every day we walk by people that we know and don't know, who are without Christ, and we don't do a thing to help them. We don't try to initiate a conversation about our faith; we just keep walking. And to be blunt, a fate even worse than a house fire awaits those who reject the offer of forgiveness through Jesus Christ. It is eternal fire.*

And the last thing that God wants is to send any man or woman—deeply loved by Him and made in His very image—to this place called Hell. That is why He sent Jesus to live a perfect life, to die a perfect death on the cross for our sins, and then to rise from the dead.

That is where you come in. God wants to use you to bring other people to Himself.

You might protest, "God could never use someone like me!" Actually He can and He will if you will let Him. It could even happen before the day is over. He will not force you to share your faith, but He will prompt you. And when you take that step of faith, He will empower and use you.

> That is where you come in. God wants to use you to bring other people to Himself.

I want you to discover the adventure of being used by God, especially in the area of telling others about Jesus.

God says He is looking for people that He can "show Himself strong on behalf of" (2 Chron. 16:9). He is searching for someone who will simply say, "Use me, Lord!" Would you be that person? If so, a wonderful adventure awaits you.

I want to let you in on what may be a surprise: sharing your faith can be both exciting and, believe it or not, fun! As Psalm 126:6 reminds us, "Those who go out weeping, carrying seed to sow, will return with songs of joy, carrying sheaves with them" (NIV).

Jesus told us there is joy in Heaven over every sinner who comes to repentance (see Luke 15:7). As C. S. Lewis pointed out, "Joy is the serious business of Heaven!"[1] So, if there is joy in Heaven upon hearing the news of a conversion, there certainly should be joy in having a role in it.

> Next to personally knowing Jesus Christ as my Savior and Lord, the greatest joy I know of is leading others to Christ and watching them grow spiritually. And you can do that too. It should be a joyful, happy thing to tell others about your relationship with God and explain how they can have one too.

Next to personally knowing Jesus Christ as my Savior and Lord, the greatest joy I know of is leading others to Christ and watching them grow spiritually. And you can do that too. It should be a joyful, happy thing to tell others about your relationship with God and explain how they can have one too.

I have found that the happiest Christians are the evangelistic ones. And I have also found that the unhappiest Christians are the nitpicky kind. They are so busy arguing theological minutia that they miss out on opportunities. As the old country preacher Vance Havner used to say, "If we are too busy using our sickles on each other, we will miss the harvest!"

Yes, there is a happiness that we are missing out on if we are not sharing our faith. John wrote that his personal joy was made complete by sharing with others the message of Christ (see 1 John 1:4). And after all, does not Scripture tell us, in Acts 20:35, "It is more blessed to give than to receive" (NLT)? Another translation of that would be, "It is more happy to give than to receive."

The believers I know who make a habit of sharing the gospel are happy people.

What's Your Excuse?

Clearly God could reach people without us, but instead He has chosen to work through us. In fact, He seems to go out of His way to find the most unlikely candidates to accomplish His divine purposes.

Think of Moses, who, when called by God to speak out for Him, essentially said, "I can't. I have a speech impediment!" (see Exod. 4:10). When called by God to speak, Jeremiah felt he was too young (see Jer. 1:6). Think of those that God used who had challenges and failures in life: Noah got drunk, Abraham was old, Jacob was a liar, and David had an affair. Peter denied Christ, the disciples fell asleep while praying, Timothy had an ulcer, and Lazarus was dead!

Again I ask, what's your excuse?

You might say, "I'm not qualified. I'm not gifted or talented." Do you want to know a little secret? You are just the person God is looking for. He likes to use people that are not necessarily self-confident. Why? Because when God does something amazing through them, He is the one who gets the glory, as He should. Paul wrote, "We now have this light shining in our hearts, but we ourselves are like fragile clay jars containing this great treasure. This makes it clear that our great power is from God, not from ourselves" (2 Cor. 4:7 NLT).

No, you may not feel qualified, but God is not looking for ability as much as He is looking for availability. God does not call the qualified; He qualifies the called.

> No, you may not feel qualified, but God is not looking for ability as much as He is looking for availability. God does not call the qualified; He qualifies the called.

There have been so many times that I have felt drained and exhausted, both physically and mentally. I have even felt like my spiritual gas tank was close to empty. But then, when I started to share the gospel with someone, or stopped thinking about myself and focused on another's needs and shared some truth from God's Word, I was replenished in every way. I started on empty and ended on full. Proverbs 11:25 tells us that "those who refresh others will themselves be refreshed" (NLT).

God has not blessed you with all the messages you have heard in church or have read in books over the years so that you can hoard it all to yourself. Have you seen the TV programs that show the lifestyle of what they call "hoarders"? I'm not talking about people who just keep a few things too long. These are people who have filled their homes, their garages, and every square inch of their space with stuff. It takes days to clear it out.

Sometimes as Christians we can be the same way—hoarding all that God has given to us, and not sharing it with others. So let's get this idea out of our heads that sharing our faith is something we cannot do and something that is miserable to engage in. Nothing could be further from the truth.

Remember this: you are blessed to be a blessing.

In this study together, we will close each chapter with prayer. The only power to change our hearts will come through our praying, like this, together:

> *"Lord, remove the excuses that bind my will from obedience to You. I am afraid, I am nervous— what if they won't listen? What if they mock me? What if they reject me? Give me all that I need to avoid the sin of not sharing the only thing that can save—Your gospel. In Jesus' name I pray, Amen."*

*To learn more about what the Bible says about Hell, go to chapter 9, "What Is the Gospel?"

CHAPTER 2

Effective Sharing Starts with Caring

People can tell if you really care about them. A child knows it; even a dog can tell! So I begin with this question: Do you care about people who do not know the Lord? Far too often we see them as the enemy when, in fact, they are under the control and influence of the real enemy, Satan.

Speaking of nonbelievers, Scripture says we are to be patient in our dealings with them. "Then they will come to their senses and escape from the devil's trap. For they have been held captive by him to do whatever he wants" (2 Tim. 2:26 NLT). So, effective sharing of one's faith starts with a concern, a burden.

I know, "Sharing starts with caring!" sounds like something cheesy like a Care Bear would say, but it's true. Effective evangelism starts with a God-given concern for the person you are speaking with.

Be Honest: How Do You Feel about Unbelievers?

The great British preacher C. H. Spurgeon wrote the following words about the unbelievers to whom we present the gospel message:

> The Holy Spirit will move them by first moving you.
> If you can rest without their being saved, they will rest
> too; but if you are filled with an agony for them, if you
> cannot bear that they should be lost, you will soon find
> that they are uneasy too. I hope you will get into such
> a state that you will dream about your child, or about
> your hearer perishing for lack of Christ, and start up at
> once and begin to cry, "O God, give me converts or I
> die!" Then you will have converts.[2]

There is even a place for anger when it comes to sharing our faith.

Before the apostle Paul delivered the gospel message to the pagans of Greece, Scripture tells us, "He was deeply troubled by all the idols" (Acts 17:16 NLT). It's no wonder. Athens was "Idol Central" of the planet at that time. Another way to translate Paul's reaction to this idolatry is, "He was irritated and aroused to anger." Have you ever looked around at our culture today, seeing so many trapped by sin, and just gotten angry? Not at the people, but at the one who is doing this to them? We usually think of anger as a negative thing, but did you know there is a place for anger? It's often called righteous indignation.

As a result of being deeply troubled, Paul came up with a plan and took action. Any effective attempt at sharing one's faith must begin with a God-given burden. Paul later wrote, "Woe to me if I do not preach the gospel!" (1 Cor. 9:16 NIV).

Now, be honest: Do you feel that way?

Spurgeon also said, "Winners of souls must first be weepers of souls."[3] If we want God to work through us to reach people who do not yet know the Lord, it must start here.

Jesus Cares

In Luke 15, we are given a perspective of how God views those who don't know Him. You may be surprised by what you read there. Jesus, in three metaphors, conveys how God loves people:

- Like a shepherd who lost a sheep. (vv. 4–7)
- Like a woman who lost a coin. (vv. 8–10)
- Like a father who lost a son. (vv. 11–32)

Have you ever lost something of great value? You search until you find it—just like the shepherd who lost his sheep. And time is of the essence for a shepherd with a wayward lamb. Sheep are defenseless animals. They cannot run fast. They do not have teeth to speak of, or even claws to scratch with. They are basically "leg of lamb" for the taking; the only thing missing is the mint sauce. Not to mention the fact that sheep are among the dumbest animals on the planet, and are constantly getting themselves into trouble. (Don't take it as a compliment when Scripture says in

Isaiah 53:6, "All we like sheep have gone astray; We have turned, every one, to his own way.")

So, in this story that Jesus told, the shepherd, despite the fact that he still has ninety-nine sheep, searches for that stray lamb until he finds it. The sheep desperately need the shepherd and the shepherd cares about his flock. When the shepherd located the lamb, he was filled with joy and brought it back, rejoicing. Jesus then inserts this point: "In the same way, there is more joy in heaven over one lost sinner who repents and returns to God than over ninety-nine others who are righteous and haven't strayed away!" (Luke 15:7 NLT).

Every time someone on earth believes in Jesus, Heaven rejoices! This reminds us that God cares about individuals. Sure, He loves the world (see John 3:16), but He loves each and every one of us—and He is searching for us.

You might say, "Yes, but that's Jesus! I just don't feel that way about people that are not Christians!"

But does not Scripture tell us, "Let this mind be in you that was also in Christ Jesus" (Phil. 2:5)?

Reflecting His love, we should be searching for others as well.

Then Jesus spoke about the woman with the lost coin. This most likely was the coin a bride would wear in her wedding headband, so it had great value on multiple levels. It would be like losing your wedding ring! My finger has grown so fat since I was married, so there is no danger of my wedding band coming off my finger. I practically need the "Jaws of Life" to get it off when I want it cleaned.

But this woman would not give up, so she searched until she found it. Again, Jesus says, "In the same way, there is joy in the presence of God's angels when even one sinner repents" (Luke 15:10 NLT).

The Father Cares

In Luke 15:11–31, we find one of the most amazing stories ever told. I have preached from this text all around the world many times, and I am always amazed at how it seems to resonate with every culture, every person—young or old, man or woman, rich or poor. It's usually referred to as the Parable of the Prodigal Son.

It is the story of a father who had two sons. In the telling of the story, we usually focus on the antics of the one boy who went, according to Jesus, "to a far country" and spent his money on wild living. He demanded from his father his portion of the inheritance, which would require the father to divide the estate at considerable cost. The boy was ungrateful and, frankly, acted like a spoiled brat. Yet, surprisingly, the father did what the son requested.

Later his older brother accused the prodigal of consorting with prostitutes, so it's clear this young man hit bottom. I'm sure when he rolled into town with all that money, he made a lot of new "friends" quickly. But when the money ran out, the friends ran out with it. This boy hit rock bottom and ended up feeding pigs (not a very kosher thing for a Jewish boy). He was so desperate, he was thinking of eating the food he fed the pigs. Then, he came to his senses and said, "My father's hired hands have it better then this. I'll just go home and tell Dad I'm not worthy to be his son, but at least I can work for him."

So, the boy began his journey home.

But let's not miss the bigger picture: this story is about the father who missed his son. Though it is referred to as the Parable of the Prodigal Son, it could just as easily be called the Parable of the Loving Father. Look at it from the father's perspective. He loved both of his sons with all of his heart. But one day, his youngest son took his money and ran. One day this boy was part of his father's life; the next day he was gone, possibly for good.

I imagine this dad would sit in his chair on the porch of his estate and just pine for that rascal of a boy. He would walk into his son's old room and memories would flood his mind of the time they spent together. There is no mention of a mother in this story, so either it was not essential to it or she was missing, perhaps due to her passing. If that was the case, this widower father was a man trying to compensate for that loss. He was clearly a good, caring, loving dad. The father was also clearly well-off financially, as he had servants, so this boy wanted for nothing.

> But let's not miss the bigger picture: this story is about the father who missed his son.

The father was affectionate as well, as shown by the dramatic conclusion to the story, when he kisses his son repeatedly. He missed that boy with all of his heart, and days turned to weeks, and weeks to months, and most likely to years. But the father never stopped loving or missing his son.

Now, here is the point: Jesus is telling us that God the Father is like the father in this story. When we or any other sinners are apart from Him, He misses us; He longs for us to return, and that is because He loves us.

Then one day it happened. Down the long road that led to the family estate, the father saw his prodigal boy. He was not as young as when he had left. Long gone was the bloom of youth, as sin had taken its toll. Perhaps he was bowed with age and his health ravaged from poor choices. But at least he was going the right direction now: toward home.

He had even written a little speech that he had memorized: "Father, I am no longer worthy to be called your son. Please just hire me on as a hand here, because your workers have it better than I do now." But when that father saw his beloved boy walking toward him, he could not contain himself. He bolted out of that chair he was sitting in and sprinted to get to him. Jesus said, "And while he was still a long way off, his father saw him coming. Filled with love and compassion, he ran to his son, embraced him, and kissed him" (Luke 15:20 NLT).

> Jesus is telling us that God the Father is like the father in this story. When we or any other sinner is apart from Him, He misses us; He longs for us to return, and that is because He loves us.

Do You Care?

Now, understand how radical of an idea this is, as conveyed by Jesus to first-century ears. In this culture, it was considered undignified for an older man to run. Not to mention that it's hard for an older man to run! (I know this from personal experience.) It could have been perceived by some to almost be an irreverent view of God the Father. But Jesus presented the Father in Heaven as willing to "lose his dignity" to get to His prodigal son! This shows how much God loves us and how much we should love those who don't yet know Him.

Would you be willing to "lose your dignity" for a moment and engage someone with the gospel message? Would you be willing to leave your "comfort zone" and take a little step of faith? Would you be honest enough to say that perhaps you don't care as much as you should about people who do not yet know the Lord? Allow me to make a suggestion. Why don't you pause for a moment before reading on, and pray a short prayer? Something along these lines:

"Lord, You have told me to go into all the world and preach the gospel. But in all honesty, I am not doing that as I should. Would You help me with this? Will You give me a heart for those that do not yet know You? Will You give me a burden for people who are not believers yet? Will You give me a holy boldness like I have never had before? I know Your heart is to reach them, and You showed this by sending Jesus to die on the cross for the sins of the world. Give me that concern for them that would reflect Your heart. In Jesus' name I pray, Amen."

CHAPTER 3

Why Share Your Faith?

Why tell others about Jesus Christ? Here is the short answer: Jesus told us to.

In fact, Jesus commanded us to take this message to the ends of the earth. Let's consider those words of the Great Commission again. As I pointed out previously, there are actually two versions of it, each complementing the other. First we have the version in Matthew's Gospel: "Go therefore and make disciples of all the nations, baptizing them in the name of the Father and of the Son and of the Holy Spirit, teaching them to observe all things that I have commanded you" (Matt. 28:19–20).

These words of Jesus are a command. It was never a mere suggestion that we, His followers, bring the gospel to others. It was, and is, as they say in the military, a direct order!

Then there is the Gospel of Mark's version of the Great Commission: "Go into all the world and preach the gospel to every creature" (Mark 16:15). So, let's put this together: the Great

Commission is to preach and teach; it is to proclaim and then disciple.

Paul writes, "We proclaim Christ! We warn everyone we meet, and we teach everyone we can, all that we know about him, so that, if possible, we may bring every man up to his full maturity in Christ" (Col. 1:28 *Phillips*). That's the objective: lead people to Jesus and bring them to maturity.

The Problem

A wonderful thing will happen to you when you have a new believer in your life: it will spiritually revive you. It is like going to Disneyland with adults versus going with children.

Adults at Disneyland tend to complain, starting with the price of admission, which is extraordinarily high. Once in the park, adults usually want to eat. Then of course they are sleepy, so they are wondering if, among Tomorrowland, Fantasyland, and all the other lands, there is such a thing as *Napland*. Adults tend to be critical, quick to point out the lack of realism in the rides, or how it was "so much better when Walt was still alive." They will also complain about how long they have to wait in line for a ride (especially when they see the sign that says, "If you are standing here you will be on the ride in . . . one month").

In contrast, try going to Disneyland with kids. It is, as the song says, "a whole new world." Kids are so excited to see the characters, experience the thrill of the rides, and visit the various lands so adeptly designed by Disney Imagineers. For children,

Disneyland really is a magical place. The favorite time for kids at Disneyland is going in; the favorite time for adults is going out.

Now, think of going to church with those who have been Christians and churchgoers for many years, even decades. You can find yourself taking things for granted, complaining, and even become somewhat jaded. The music is too loud. The music is not loud enough. The church is too small. The church is too big. The pastor's sermons are too long. The pastor's sermons are too short. You don't like it when the pastor adds a call for people to come to Christ at the end of the service because you have "heard all that before" and besides, you want to go to lunch! The list of complaints continues.

A Solution

I have a solution for you: take a nonbeliever or a newly minted believer to church with you next Sunday. I guarantee you will hear and see things far differently when you bring a visitor. If they are not yet a Christian, you will find yourself praying fervently for the pastor's message and hope he extends that invitation for people to come to Christ. And if that person you brought does believe in Jesus, now you have the privilege and joy of helping them get on their feet and reach spiritual maturity.

Like taking a child to Disneyland, when you have a new believer in tow, you see and hear things in a new way—through their eyes, so to speak. Watch them process the Word of God for the first time and discover the joy of worship. It can revitalize you! And those amazing conversations after church as they ask you countless questions about what passages from Scripture mean. You realize, for starters, that you know a lot more than you think you did. All that time listening to Bible studies and studying on your own has paid huge dividends. And for those questions you do not have the answer to, you can go to the pastor or a more mature Christian for their insight—and, of course, you can search the Scriptures on your own.

No doubt about it, new believers are the lifeblood of the church. They also are the lifeblood of the Christian. We all need a new believer in our life. We need to deepen and ground them. In turn, they reignite and excite us.

You show me a church that does not have a constant flow of new Christians coming in, and I will show you a church that is stagnating. We in the church have a choice: evangelize or fossilize! The same could be said for us as individuals as well.

Another thing about these words of the Great Commission to both preach the gospel and make disciples: they are directed to every follower of Jesus. These words were not merely directed to the original disciples. Nor are they meant only for what we might call "professionals"—evangelists, pastors, missionaries, etc. They are for *every follower* of Jesus. Every man and every woman who believes in Him is called and commanded to go and proclaim His message.

My First Opportunity

I have to admit, when my first opportunity came to share my newfound faith, I did not do very well. I was seventeen years old and I was hanging around a motley crew. As Garth Brooks sang, I had "friends in low places." My buddies and I would get high on weed pretty much every day. Much of this happened at a friend's house not far from my high school, where I had just accepted Christ.

I had not seen or spoken with these guys since I asked the Lord into my life, so I thought I would see what they were up to. On my way over, one of the Christians from my campus recognized me and loudly yelled, "Hey, Brother Greg!"

Who is this guy, and why is he calling me Brother *Greg*? I wondered. The excited Christian came over and gave me a big hug and told me he saw me walk forward and pray with the other students days before at the Bible study on the front lawn. I reluctantly admitted that it was true, wondering why he was asking. He then pulled out a very large, well-worn Bible and thrust it into my hands, exclaiming, "Then you need a Bible, bro! Here, take mine!"

Really just wanting him to go away, I reluctantly agreed and took the Bible. I must tell you, this was not just a big Bible, but one that had been "customized." It had a weathered suede cover with two Popsicle sticks glued on the front, forming a cross. Being a designer, this was somewhat of an assault on my ascetic sense in addition to being so gigantic. I was not quite prepared to carry it around. So I shoved the massive Bible with Popsicle sticks forming a cross into my outer coat pocket, ripping the pocket in the process. Needless to say, I was hardly proud of my commitment at this point.

So I went to see my friends in the home that I used to frequent to get high, and they were all there as usual. As I was making my way in, I suddenly remembered my giant Bible in my ripped pocket, so I pulled it out and hid it in the bushes in a planter in front of the house and then walked in. The last thing I wanted at that point was questions about it.

Every eye turned to me, and one of my buddies called out, "Laurie! Where have you been?"

"Nowhere special," I said, clearly evading the truth.

"What have you been up to? We haven't seen you for a while," another said.

"I haven't been up to anything!" I said, getting defensive.

"We have some new weed. Want to get high?"

"No!" I said loudly. Now they knew something was different about me. I was clearly feeling uncomfortable.

Suddenly, the front door bursts open and it's the mother of my friend, holding my Bible! "Who does this belong to?" she shouts, as though she just found illegal contraband. I thought, *This woman has kids doing drugs in her house every day and here she's visibly upset at the discovery of a copy of the Bible in her planter?*

It's a funny thing, but everyone in that room looked at that Bible and then they looked at me. They somehow knew there was a connection. And there was my Popsicle-cross Bible on open display.

"Uh, that's mine," I sheepishly replied, reaching up and taking it into my hands.

"What is that, Laurie?" one of my friends asked.

"It's a Bible," I said as quietly as possible, wanting this conversation to end.

"A what?" another asked loudly.

"A Bible!" I shouted back.

Now, my buddies, even though high, figured out what had happened to me.

"Oh, are we going to be Christians now, reading the Bible and praising God?" one mockingly said.

"No, I'm going to hit you in the mouth if you don't shut up!" I said back. (I had not read 1 Corinthians 13 yet.)

They began to laugh and mock and pile it on, clearly enjoying my discomfort. I stormed out of the house, with my Popsicle-cross Bible, and realized for the first time that my old life was over and I had failed miserably in my first opportunity to share my faith.

I would try to be better prepared next time.

———

In the Great Commission, we are commanded by Jesus to go and verbally communicate His Good News of salvation to as many people as we can. If they respond to this message, we are to "make disciples" of them. That is, we are to help them to be grounded in their faith and be integrated into a local church. Then, we are to go and repeat this process.

Though my first opportunity to *Tell Someone* didn't go very well, it didn't have to be my last. If you're anything like me, your first opportunity doesn't have to be your last either. Let's pray together:

"*Lord, as we go into all the world to share the gospel,
help us to be strong when we face discouragement,
ridicule, and even suffering. We know these pale in
comparison to Jesus' humiliation on the cross. You have
shown us the strength, even until death, to endure even
the worst blunders. Go with us, as we go in obedience
to Your commands. In Jesus' name I pray, Amen.*"

CHAPTER 4

Where to Preach the Gospel?

Now let's consider where we should share the gospel. Short answer: everywhere!

Back to the words of Jesus: "Go into all the world!" Let me personalize that for you: go into all of *your* world. Every one of us has a sphere of influence: people we work with, live by, and engage daily.

- Go into all of your family and preach the gospel.
- Go into all of your workplace and preach the gospel.
- Go into all of your neighborhood and preach the gospel.
- Go into all of your world and preach the gospel.

Perhaps you have a neighbor who really gets on your nerves, and you would rather not preach the gospel to them. Or a coworker who is really irritating—possibly even someone you regard as an enemy. Take the gospel to them too!

After all, did not Jesus tell us to love our enemies? What better way to love them than to tell them how to go to Heaven? President Abraham Lincoln once said, "The best way to destroy an enemy is make him a friend."

Are You Running?

If you have a hard time thinking about taking the gospel to someone you dislike, you are not alone. The prophet Jonah had the same issue. God told him to go to the Ninevites and preach to them, as He was soon going to judge them. Jonah, being a patriotic Israelite, did not want to go to his enemies with a message of hope and forgiveness from God. Knowing God's nature, he was concerned that God would pardon them if they repented, so he figured, if he did not go to them they could not repent.

As far as Jonah was concerned, he would prefer God destroy the people of Nineveh. That would be one less enemy for Israel to be concerned with. So he boarded a ship and went the opposite direction to a place called Tarshish.

To sum things up,

God said, "Go!"

Jonah said, "No!"

God said, "Oh?"

Know this: the Lord will always have the last word. You probably know the rest of the story: a great storm overcame Jonah's ship, and he was thrown overboard and swallowed by a massive fish, perhaps a whale. (The word in Hebrew is actually "sea monster".) There in the belly of the beast after three days of stubborn rebellion, Jonah finally came to his senses. He repented of his sin and stubbornness and was recommissioned by God. And that sea creature came to the shore of the place the Lord originally told Jonah to go and vomited him there.

There was no getting out of this, as far as the Lord was concerned. It was "Nineveh or bust!" So Jonah was repentant and regurgitated. Believing and barfed. Righteous and ralphed. Right on the shore of the nation he did not want to go to. He was the right man, at the right place, at the right time—albeit with a bit of an odor to him.

Is there someone that the Lord has been nudging you to engage with the gospel? Are you running from that, or are you doing what God is telling you to do?

There for a Purpose

One of my favorite stories in the Old Testament is of the strikingly beautiful Jewish girl named Hadassah. She entered a nationwide beauty contest staged by the king of Persia. The winner would become the next queen of the kingdom. Hadassah won and became known as Queen Esther.

Her story initially reads as a fairy tale, until it took a very dark turn. A villain even more sinister than any child's story would produce emerges with a plan to exterminate the Jewish people. His name was Haman. He gets the king to unwittingly sign a decree that all the Jews in the kingdom would be put to death. This would also include the Hebrew queen. But at this point, Queen Esther was disconnected from the needs of her people, as she lived a life of pampered luxury in the safety and comfort of the royal palace.

So, her cousin Mordecai covered himself in sackcloth and stood outside the palace. Alerted to this, the queen sent him a change of clothes. Talk about missing the point! She was oblivious to the plight of her people until her cousin sends her the following message:

> "If you keep quiet at a time like this, deliverance and
> relief for the Jews will arise from some other place,
> but you and your relatives will die. Who knows if
> perhaps you were made queen for just such a time as
> this?" (Esther 4:14 NLT)

Allow me to loosely paraphrase this statement: "Esther, you are not where you are by coincidence but by providence. You are in a position to potentially save your people. If you don't do it, God will find someone else. But did it ever occur to you that you are where you are for this very moment?"

Now, let me apply that to you, and to myself. We can be just like Queen Esther, happily ensconced in the security of the church and surrounded by our Christian friends, as we watch Christian movies and eat in Christian restaurants and read Christian books. We can seek to live in a Christian bubble and have little to no contact with the real world of lost people. But we are missing amazing opportunities to be used by God.

God wants you to go into all of your world and preach the gospel! Jesus did not say that the whole world should go to church, but He did say that the church should go to the whole world. Esther was placed where she was "for such a time as this," and so are you.

Did it ever occur to you that you are right where God wants you to be? That irritating neighbor and the disagreeable coworker have been put in your life so you can reach them with the message of the gospel! You are there for a purpose.

> God wants you to go into all of your world and preach the gospel!

Why don't you start by praying for them? It's hard to continue to think of a person as an enemy when you pray for them. Instead of trying to wiggle out of where you are, why not look for "divine appointments." You are where you are "for such a time as this."

> That irritating neighbor and the disagreeable coworker have been put in your life so you can reach them with the message of the gospel!

Bridge or Barrier

Back to Jonah. On the shores of Nineveh, he began to preach the message the Lord gave him. I'm not quite sure why Jonah ran from God in the first place. Perhaps he was afraid of rejection. You could say he was the original "chicken of the sea." I think perhaps what he really feared was success. In other words, he was afraid God would spare them, and that is exactly what the Lord did.

But instead of rejoicing at their repentance, Jonah was angry. The Bible tells us, "So he complained to the LORD about it:

'Didn't I say before I left home that you would do this, LORD? That is why I ran away to Tarshish! I knew that you are a merciful and compassionate God, slow to get angry and filled with unfailing love. You are eager to turn back from destroying people'" (Jonah 4:2 NLT).

So much for the idea of the "wrathful God" of the Old Testament as compared to the "loving God" of the New Testament. There is only one true God in the Bible, and He is holy, righteous, and perfect. He also is loving, forgiving, and ready to pardon. That's because God loves and cares for lost people, and so should we.

It could be that the reason we don't want to share our faith is the deep-seated fear that the person we speak with will indeed respond and make a commitment to follow Christ. Why? Because we know it is our responsibility to then take them under our wing and help integrate them into our church—and in all honesty, that could be quite the inconvenience.

> It could be that the reason we don't want to share our faith is the deep-seated fear that the person we speak with will indeed respond and make a commitment to follow Christ.

There are some Christians who don't necessarily want a new Christian hanging around them, because some choices in their lives might be a potential stumbling block to the new believer and, frankly, they don't want that kind of pressure. But that is exactly why you should have a new believer around! It jars you from a complacency you have drifted into. Is that not a good thing?

Let me ask you, are you a stepping-stone or a stumbling block? Are you a bridge or a barrier to people coming to know Jesus Christ? You will find that you are either one or the other.

> Are you a stepping-stone or a stumbling block? Are you a bridge or a barrier to people coming to know Jesus Christ? You will find that you are either one or the other.

Live the Gospel or Preach the Gospel?

The answer to the question is, "Yes."

Jonah was called to go and preach to the people of Nineveh, and we have been called to go to our world as well.

Some will set up a false dichotomy and say something along the lines of, "I don't really feel comfortable *preaching*. I will just be a good example and win people to Christ through the way I live." But Jesus did not say to merely, "Go into all the world and be a good example." He said, "Go into all the world and preach the gospel."

Don't misunderstand what I am stating here; you don't want to be a bad example. Nothing hurts our presentation of the gospel more than contradicting what we say by the way that we live.

It's been said, "There are two reasons people don't go to church: 1) They don't know a Christian, and 2) They do know a Christian!"

> "There are two reasons people don't go to church: 1) They don't know a Christian, and 2) They do know a Christian!"

You get the drift; hypocrisy undermines our evangelistic efforts like nothing else. It won't be long when sharing your faith before someone says to you, "The reason I am not a Christian is because there are too many hypocrites in the church!" Now, granted, that may be more of an excuse than a reason, but we know that they have a point as well.

Clearly, before you can effectively preach it, you must first live it. Billy Graham once said, "We are the Bibles the world is reading. We are the creeds the world is needing. We are the sermons the world is heeding."[4] Christians are walking epistles, written by God and read by men.

We need people today who walk the walk, as well as talk the talk. People who, before they speak a single word, give evidence that there is something different about them. We need people who, through their godly lifestyles, have earned the right to be heard.

> We need people today who walk the walk, as well as talk the talk.

So, this is not a choice between simply being a good example of a follower of Jesus or preaching to others but not living it. We want to model it and preach it. It's not "either/or" but rather "both/and."

To help us understand how both example and proclamation work together, let's consider the words of Jesus in what is regarded as the greatest sermon ever preached, the Sermon on the Mount. There, Jesus told us that we are to be "the salt of the earth" and to "let our lights shine" (see Matt. 5:13, 16).

In the first century, salt was used, among other things, to stop putrefaction in meat. It would be rubbed in meat to keep it edible. This was long before the days of refrigeration. So, with this in mind, Jesus says that we as Christians should be salt, meaning we should do what we can to stop the spread of evil.

We speak out for those who cannot speak for themselves, we try to right wrongs, we stand up for what is true. Hopefully, we live in such a way that our very presence as followers of Jesus affects those around us. For instance, just as your coworkers are telling that dirty joke, you come walking in and the joke stops. Why? Because you are a representative of Jesus Christ! You are being "salt" in that situation as Jesus told you to be.

What's sad is if those people telling the dirty joke continue on after you walk in and you already know the punch line! I met a guy in the gym a while back and we were talking. He was using a lot of profanity and someone interrupted him and said, "Do you realize that Greg is a pastor?" Clearly embarrassed, the guy turned red and said to me, "Pardon my French, Reverend!" Man, I have never heard French like that before!

> I don't expect non-Christians to act and speak like Christians. I expect them to be "true to form," and I am there to build a bridge, not burn one.

You might be surprised to know I did not jump down this guy's throat. That's because I don't expect non-Christians to act and speak like Christians. I expect them to be "true to form," and I am there to build a bridge, not burn one. Having said that, his knowing that

I was a representative of Jesus Christ stopped him from something he was doing that was wrong. That's a good thing.

Christians are the ones that speak out for what is right and against what is wrong, and so we should. But salt not only stops the spread of putrefaction; it also stimulates thirst. You know how that works. You go to the movie and buy some popcorn. What is the deal with the portion sizes in theaters these days? "Small" is a tiny little bag, "medium" is slightly bigger, and "large" is the size of a trashcan! Who needs that much popcorn? So, you go with the larger size because it's a better deal (even though you have to finance it), and go into your movie and munch away. Then you notice it's heavily salted, so now you have to go back and buy a five-gallon bucket of Coke to quench your thirst.

The salt has done its work: it has stimulated your thirst.

> One of the greatest compliments we can be paid by a nonbeliever is when they say something like, "I notice that you have a joy and a peace in life. Despite the fact that you have had hardships, you keep smiling. What is your secret?"

One of the greatest compliments we can be paid by a nonbeliever is when they say something like, "I notice that you have a joy and a peace in life. Despite the fact that you have had hardships, you keep smiling. What is your secret?"

What a great way to start a presentation of the gospel! That's what happened to me as I watched that godly young girl on my high school campus who believed in Jesus. She was being salt and she brought me to the light.

Songs in the Night

That is what happened to Paul and Silas, who were put in prison for preaching the gospel. The jailer was especially cruel, whipping them and then throwing them into an inner dungeon and putting their feet in stocks. Yet these two disciples were rejoicing and singing. What a powerful testimony it is when a Christian can praise God despite hard circumstances.

Any fool can be happy when the sun is shining and the skies are blue. But when the bottom drops out of life and you can still give thanks to God—that is going to impact people. And indeed it did. The story tells us that "around midnight Paul and Silas were praying and singing hymns to God, and the other prisoners were listening" (Acts 16:25 NLT). The word used for *listening* means "to listen with pleasure." It is doubtful those other prisoners had ever heard anything like this before.

Then a mighty earthquake struck and the prison walls broke apart, and the chains of the prisoners came off, making it possible for them to escape. When the cruel Roman jailer saw this, he pulled out his short sword that the Romans used for close combat and he was getting ready to kill himself. The reason for this is that if these prisoners escaped, the Roman soldier would be executed. So he figured he would just take care of it himself.

Suddenly, the apostle Paul stopped him, shouting, "Stop! Don't kill yourself! We are all here!" (Acts 16:28 NLT). This hardened jailer could not believe his ears or eyes. He was so moved by this, and the powerful testimony of Paul and Silas rejoicing before this, that he was ready to believe right there on the spot, saying "What must I do to be saved?" (v. 30 NLT).

Paul and Silas earned the right to be heard. Their actions paved the way for their message.

You Are Being Watched

If we are not being the salt Jesus wants us to be, we are not fulfilling the purpose for which God made us. There is nothing more useless than "unsalty" salt. It's like ordering a Coke that has lost its carbonation. What good is it? Jesus said, "You are the salt of the earth. But what good is salt if it has lost its flavor? Can you make it salty again? It will be thrown out and trampled underfoot as worthless" (Matt. 5:13 NLT).

You are being watched by nonbelievers. They are often wanting—even hoping—you will slip up or do something inconsistent so they can hide behind their argument, "The church is full of hypocrites." I urge you to defy their expectations.

> You are being watched by nonbelievers. They are often wanting—even hoping—you will slip up or do something inconsistent so they can hide behind their argument, "The church is full of hypocrites." I urge you to defy their expectations.

Seek to be a good example as a follower of Christ, and look for that opportunity to engage people with the message of the gospel.

I was in a Starbucks with a friend of mine named Marty. He ordered a "small, soy, decaf latte." I turned to Marty and said, "What's the point? All the fun is gone! Why don't you just hold an empty cup and pretend to drink?" The problem today is that we have too many "decaf disciples," too many "uncarbonated Christians."

You see, being a good example as a follower of Jesus Christ is not enough. Jesus told us to go and preach His gospel. By the way, to "preach" does not mean you have to speak loudly or stand on a platform. You can preach in a conversational way, engaging your listener. Again, the point is verbal communication of the gospel message that has already been lived out before their eyes.

You might say, "I am not really comfortable talking with strangers." I understand that, but consider this: the primary way God has chosen to reach people is through other people. And the primary way He works through people is through the verbalization of the gospel. The Bible asks, "How can they hear about him unless someone *tells them*?" (Rom. 10:14 NLT, italics added).

> The primary way God has chosen to reach people is through other people. And the primary way He works through people is through the verbalization of the gospel.

Let's say you were a brilliant scientist who had become a victim of cancer, so you dedicated your life and considerable skills to finding a way to bring an end to this dreaded disease for both yourself and others. Then one day, you finally found the cure. You simplified the treatment to one single pill that, if taken once, the cancer would disappear immediately. What would you do with such a discovery?

I hope you would shout it from the rooftops and tell everyone everywhere. Would you say, "Well, I'm not really comfortable talking to people I don't know, so I really don't want to do that!" No, that would be criminal, to say the least.

To quote C. H. Spurgeon again, "If sinners be damned, at least let them leap to Hell over our dead bodies. And if they perish, let them perish with our arms wrapped about their knees, imploring them to stay. If Hell must be filled, let it be filled in the teeth of our exertions, and let not one go unwarned and unprayed for."[5]

How much more should we who are Christians feel the compulsion to overcome our fears and share this gospel message with as many people as possible? We have something even more important than the cure for cancer, as wonderful as that would be. We have the "cure" for eternal separation from God. We'll talk more about that in later chapters, but for now let's come back to the word *gospel*.

That word means "Good News." Would it seem strange if you turned on the evening news and the anchorman just sat there? Perhaps he was doing the best job he could as an example of a good anchorman. No, that anchorman is there to deliver the news, and that requires verbal communication. We are to do the same—but our message is eternal and it is urgently needed.

The gospel is only Good News if it gets there in time.

―――――――

"Lord, give us the courage to Tell Someone everywhere we go. Let our presence in the world enhance every place we inhabit. Give us the saltiness the world needs to call out to You. Grant us the power both to live the gospel, and preach the gospel. In Jesus' name I pray, Amen."

―――――――

CHAPTER 5

When Should We Share the Gospel?

I wish I could tell you that every day God wakes me up and speaks to me audibly about who I am to go to. (Cue *Mission Impossible* theme song.)

"Good morning, Greg. Your mission, should you choose to accept it, is to go to a man named Josh Smith who will be pumping gas near your house at the corner gas station at 11:02. Go share the gospel with him. This message will self-destruct in five seconds."

No, that is not how the Lord leads me, or anyone else for that matter. The more likely scenario is that my "idiot light" on my car's gas gauge will go on, indicating that I am running low on fuel. So I pull over to the nearest gas station, which "happens" to be on the corner by my house. There, as I am pumping gas, is a guy next to me doing the same. I strike up a conversation, and before I know it, I realize it is a divine appointment.

When should we share the Good News of Jesus Christ? Short answer: whenever!

It is a good thing to go out with the express purpose of telling others about Christ, but we must always be available to the prompting of the Holy Spirit. The Bible says we are to "be ready in season and out of season" (2 Tim. 4:2), or in other words, "Be on duty at all times!"

Go into All the World, Even the Restroom

Some years ago, I was in a department store in a mall and I had to use the bathroom. Once seated, I heard a man clear his throat in the stall next to me. We were the only ones in the restroom. After a few moments, that same man said to me, "Hi!"

Please understand, I do not normally talk to people in public restrooms. My objective is to get in and out as quickly as possible. I shot back, "Uh . . . Hi," as curtly as I could. Another moment passed, and the guy says, "Do you have something for me?" I could not believe this conversation. Who was this person? What was he up to? I firmly said, "No, I do not!"

"Oh," he responded, clearly disappointed. Then my curiosity was piqued. I asked, "Why, what are you looking for exactly?"

"I was going to buy some drugs," he sheepishly responded. Then it occurred to me. Could this possibly be a divine appointment? Would God want me to actually share the gospel through a stall wall in a . . . public restroom? I was game, so I said, "I don't have drugs, but I have something far better for you!"

He seemed excited, "What?"

"A personal relationship with God through Jesus Christ!" I said. Then I thought, *What am I doing? You can't share the gospel in a bathroom stall!* There was a moment of silence, and he said, "Oh, I already tried that."

I was surprised. "Really? Did you ever go to a church?" He then said, "Yes, I went to Harvest Christian Fellowship." Oh, this was indeed a divine appointment.

"Do you know who I am?" I said. "I'm Greg Laurie, the pastor of Harvest Christian Fellowship."

There was a moment of silence, and he then said, "Oh my God!" I had to laugh. I said, "Buddy, God must really love you. Here you are trying to make a drug buy and the Lord sends your pastor to deter you." I went on to tell him he needed to make a recommitment to follow Christ.

I was tired of bathroom ministry, so I told him to meet me outside, in the sock department, which was nearby. He was easy to spot; he was the guilty looking guy walking out. We then prayed together and he made a recommitment to follow Jesus Christ!

No question, this was an appointment with God, for both this young man and myself. And in a men's restroom of all places! Understand, I'm not necessarily encouraging you to strike up conversations in such a place, but what I am saying is, always be ready. You never know when the Lord will call on you.

"Lord, prepare opportunities in our path to share the gospel on time. Conform our wills to bend to Yours in someone else's time of need. Prepare the hearts of our hearers to be receptive to your Good News. Make us ready. Make us willing. In Jesus' name I pray, Amen."

CHAPTER 6

The How-To
(Jesus-Style Evangelism)

Now, let's move to the "how" question, as in, how do we go about sharing the gospel?

Let's begin by pointing out our objective. As I have already stated, our goal is to build a bridge to our listener, not burn one.

I have seen Christians armed with memorized Bible verses and clever arguments completely overwhelm a person in a "gospel barrage." They may have even won the debate, but sadly they did not win the soul.

One of the best ways to share your faith is to engage a person. You don't have to necessarily hit them with the whole message up front. In fact, the more you know about the person you are speaking with, the better. Know this: everyone's favorite subject is themselves. After all, what is the most popular kind of photo today? Selfies, of course!

Ask a person questions about their life, their views, their outlook. What do they think about this or that? Don't interrupt them. Instead, try to understand what they are saying. Then, lovingly begin to build your bridge to them.

> I have seen Christians armed with memorized Bible verses and clever arguments completely overwhelm a person in a "gospel barrage." They may have even won the debate, but sadly they did not win the soul.

How Jesus Went

There is no better example of this than Jesus Christ Himself. He was God in human form, walking among us. He is the Savior of the world. But He also is the Master Communicator, showing us by example how to engage people. The template for one-on-one evangelism is found in the fourth chapter of the Gospel of John.

The woman we find there is best known simply as "the woman at the well." This woman had lived a sad and wasted life. She did not know the Scriptures. She was not educated. She had made a lot of bad moral decisions in life, being married and divorced five times. Add to that the fact that she was living with a man at present. That was extremely scandalous at that point in history.

Yet Jesus did not condemn; He reached out to her. He showed us how to be a stairway, not a stumbling block—how to be a bridge instead of a barrier to people coming to Christ.

No wonder He was called "the friend of sinners." The Bible tells us she drew her water at 12:00 noon—the hottest part of the day. That's because she was not welcome in the early morning hours, when the other women of the village would draw their water and catch up on the latest town gossip. No, she was isolated and alone—a social pariah.

Quite frankly, she reminds me of my own mother when she was on her search for meaning in her life. My mom even managed to surpass this woman in marriages: the woman at the well was divorced five times while my mother was divorced seven times, and lived with many men between the marriages. I ought to know; I was there with a front-row seat.

> Yet Jesus did not condemn; He reached out to her. He showed us how to be a stairway, not a stumbling block—how to be a bridge instead of a barrier to people coming to Christ.

I'm sure this woman was physically attractive. But with the passing of the years, that once legendary beauty was starting to fade. Men had used and abused her, no doubt. At least the prior men had married her; now she gives it away for free as she lives with a man.

Add to that a gloom that overtook her as she became hardened by the sin she lived in, and the repercussions that came as a result. Sin had effectively chewed her up and spit her out. I'm guessing she was very cynical about men in general, as she had been so mistreated by them over the years.

But a man was now going to change her life. Not just any man. She was going to meet the God-Man, Jesus Christ. Although she was not aware of it, she had an appointment with Him on that hot, sunny day. In fact, the story tells us that Jesus "needed to go" to where she was (John 4:4), not because Samaria was on His way to where He was going. In fact, it was quite out of the way. More to the point, Jewish people as a rule did not go to Samaria because of the long-standing conflict between Jews and Samaritans. They were enemies. But in contrast to Jonah, who did not want to preach to his enemies, Jesus did.

Jesus "needed to go" because there was a burned-out, hurting woman who needed His help. And God always keeps His appointments. In fact, His appointments are often found in our disappointments.

> Jesus "needed to go" because there was a burned-out, hurting woman who needed His help. And God always keeps His appointments. In fact, His appointments are often found in our disappointments.

And this woman, coming to draw water, was disappointed in life. As she approached the well, wiping the sweat from her brow, she saw a surprising sight. There, sitting at the well, was an outsider. A stranger. A Jewish man. She braced herself for a confrontation. But much to her surprise, this man, Jesus Christ, asked her a question: "Can I have a drink of water?"

What a disarming question that was for Jesus to ask. He was showing His humanity, even a tender vulnerability. He was appealing to her curiosity, to her inner spiritual thirst. This conveys an important principle when we are establishing initial contact with a nonbeliever: don't come off as a "holier than thou" know-it-all. Have a little humility.

Remember, you and I are just beggars telling another beggar where to find food. We are not superior to anyone else. Better-off perhaps, but not better.

> Remember, you and I are just beggars telling another beggar where to find food. We are not superior to anyone else. Better-off perhaps, but not better.

Spiritual Chumming

She thought this was some kind of attempt to engage in debate, and she responded, "Why would you, a Jewish man, ask for a drink of water from me, a Samaritan woman? Don't you know that Jews have no dealings with Samaritans?"

Jesus' answer to her statement is really Evangelism 101. Jesus told Simon Peter that if he would follow Him, he would become a "fisher of men." Clearly Jesus is fishing here as He seeks to engage her, even throwing out a little bait in hopes that she will take a bite. Jesus replied, "If you only knew the gift God has for you and who you are speaking to, you would ask me, and I would give you living water" (John 4:10 NLT).

This is a great way to engage a person. Make a spiritual point, and see if they respond. In fishing terms, it's called "chumming." That's when you throw some bait or other things into the water to attract fish.

I read a story of a man who was bitten by a great white shark. He was out swimming when the beast bit him. But something that came out later was that this man had been chumming off the pier first, trying to attract sharks. Careful what you wish for; you might get it.

There are a lot of ways one can chum. Perhaps mention that God answered a prayer for you or blessed you, or say something like, "It's amazing to realize that the Bible predicted so many of the things that are happening in our world right now!"

That's chumming—throwing out the bait. Sometimes people will ignore you. Other times they may respond, "What do you mean by that?"

I have a friend named Steve who will often say to people, "Has anyone ever told you that there is a God in Heaven who loves you?" You would think people might be irritated to hear such a question. I will admit, Steve has posed this question in some pretty awkward situations, like asking the barista in a coffee place with ten people behind him in line. But people are generally delighted to hear such a thing, and it certainly has opened some doors for some fascinating conversations, even resulting in people committing their lives to Christ.

As Jesus makes this statement, the Samaritan woman is intrigued, and she also is cynical. She sarcastically says to Jesus, "But sir, you don't have a rope or a bucket . . . and this well is very deep. Where would you get this living water? And besides, do you think you're greater than our ancestor Jacob, who gave us this well? How can you offer better water than he and his sons and his animals enjoyed?" (John 4:11–12 NLT).

Imagine how Jesus could have answered this statement. Was He "greater" than Jacob? He *created* Jacob, and everyone else for that matter! But that certainly would have been too much too soon for this woman. So instead He continued to appeal to her curiosity. Jesus replied, "Anyone who drinks this water will soon become thirsty again. But those who drink the water I give will never be thirsty again. It becomes a fresh, bubbling spring within them, giving them eternal life" (John 4:13–14 NLT).

Now Jesus was using the water this woman drew from the well as a metaphor for life in general. "Anyone who drinks this water will soon become thirsty again." You could write that over the "wells" that so many drink from today:

The well of the accumulation of material things
The well of success
The well of pleasure
The well of sex
The well of *whatever*

"Anyone who drinks this water will soon become thirsty again." In this woman's case, Jesus was referring to the fact that she had come to the "well" of relationships and sex five times and found no satisfaction. She was still being quite flippant when she, I think sarcastically, shot back, "Please, sir, . . . give me this water! Then I'll never be thirsty again, and I won't have to come here to get water" (v. 15).

> Now Jesus puts His finger on that black spot in her life. "Go and get your husband," Jesus told her.

"I don't have a husband," the woman replied.

Jesus said, "You're right! You don't have a husband—for you have had five husbands, and you aren't even married to the man you're living with now. You certainly spoke the truth!" (John 4:16–18 NLT)

Bingo! Jesus now has traction and His words hit the intended target. The woman is stunned that this stranger knows so much about her. "'Sir,' the woman said, 'you must be a prophet'!" (v. 19 NLT). He has seen through her façade and has her number.

My "God Drawer"

I remember before I was a Christian, I would hang around on the streets of the beachside town of Newport Beach, where I grew up. I would hide behind my façade like this woman, with the toughest look on my face I could muster. I did this when I saw the Christians coming my way, armed with their Bibles and evangelistic tracts. Apparently my act worked, because they would occasionally thrust one of their tracts in my direction but never engage me in conversation.

> Inside I was saying, *Don't buy this tough-guy persona! Talk to me about God!* But I was too proud to ask. I wanted to know more about Him, but no one would ever tell me.

Inside I was saying, *Don't buy this tough-guy persona! Talk to me about God!* But I was too proud to ask. I wanted to know more about Him, but no one would ever tell me.

As stated before, Scripture tells us "How can they call on him to save them unless they believe in him? And how can they believe in him if they have never heard about him? And how can they hear about him unless someone tells them?" (Rom. 10:14 NLT).

This may surprise you: I never threw one of those religious booklets away. I acted like I did not care, and I'd grab them out of the hands of the people giving them out and shove them in my pocket, but the fact is I saved every one, keeping them in a drawer in my bedroom. It was sort of my "God drawer." Every now and then, I would empty the contents of the drawer onto my bed and try to make sense of it. I really wanted to know how to know God.

There was literature from Christians, as well as Jehovah's Witnesses, Mormons, Hare Krishnas . . . you name it. All of these booklets referenced God but they seemed to contradict each other. And indeed they did—because all religions do not teach the same thing, as some would assert.

I needed someone to tell me and show me the way.

Show Them the Way

This reminds me of the biblical story of a man of great importance who came to the city of Jerusalem looking for truth. Instead of the vibrant faith of the former glory days of Jewish history, he found a dead, lifeless orthodoxy. But this foreign dignitary, no doubt because of his importance, did leave the city with something of great value: a personal copy of the scroll of Isaiah the prophet.

Scripture tells us he was the treasurer for the Queen of Ethiopia, so he probably traveled in a caravan with a large entourage. As he left Jerusalem, he was riding in his chariot, reading out loud from Isaiah chapter 53, trying to make some rhyme or reason out of it. Fact is, Isaiah 53 prophetically speaks of the suffering of the Messiah hundreds of years before it happened. And God had the right man in the right place at the right time to intercept him and answer this spiritually hungry man's questions. Talk about divine appointments.

The man God chose was a follower of Jesus named Philip, and he had just been directed by the Lord to go to the desert and wait. No detailed blueprint. No battle plan. God directed him to just go to the desert and wait. That is how God usually leads us: one step at a time.

Philip may have been frustrated, standing in the blazing sun and wondering how this was a good idea—that is, until he saw this large caravan approaching with this foreign dignitary, identified as the Ethiopian eunuch, reading aloud from Isaiah's book. Now, Philip did something that is very important when it comes to sharing your faith: he said the right thing at the right time.

Philip used something that is missing in many evangelistic endeavors: tact. *Tact* has been defined as "the intuitive knowledge of saying the right thing at the right time."

Other words for tact are *diplomacy, sensitivity,* and *savoir faire.* Tact is simply skill and grace in dealing with others. Isaac Newton said, "Tact is the art of making a point without making an enemy."

Philip tactfully asked the man from Ethiopia, "Do you understand what you are reading?" Philip did not push himself on this man; he asked him a simple and straightforward question. Much to his delight, the dignitary responded, "How can I, unless someone instructs me?" (literally "Show me the way"). And then he "urged Philip to come up into the carriage and sit with him" (Acts 8:31 NLT).

> Philip used something that is missing in many evangelistic endeavors: tact. *Tact* has been defined as "the intuitive knowledge of saying the right thing at the right time."

From that point, Philip explained the Scriptures to this searching man, and it resulted in his conversion that day. He was even baptized on the spot! The man needed someone to instruct him— to show him the way. I love the way the story ends. We read that the man from Ethiopia "went on his way rejoicing" (Acts 8:39 NLT).

That's all I was searching for: someone to show me the way. A poll by researcher George Barna revealed that about 25 percent of the adults in the United States would go to church if a friend would just invite them. Barna elaborated, "The best chance of getting them to a church is when someone they know and trust invites them and offers to accompany them."[6] That is really an amazing statistic. Think about it for a moment: 25 percent of the people out there are waiting for an invitation to go to church.

Do you have friends?
Do you have friends who are not believers?

Do you have nonbelieving friends you haven't invited to
   church?

The key is to invite them. And more to the point, you pick
them up and take them with you. Even if the pastor does not
extend an invitation for people to come to Christ in the service,
you could go out for lunch afterward and have that conversation
with them.

Most people come to faith because someone shares the gospel
with them.

The "Jesus Style" of Evangelism

Back to Jesus and the woman at the well. Notice that Jesus
did not start out with some question like, "Are you saved?" or,
"Did you know you're going to Hell?" No, that was not Jesus'
style. This was a dialogue, not a monologue. He spoke and He
listened. That's the "Jesus style" of evangelism, and it should be
ours as well.

Some Christians are robotic in their speaking to people, and
that will always result in a complete disconnect. Others are like
"evangelism machines," trying to talk to as many people as they
can in one day. God wants sharpshooters, not machine-gunners.

In contrast, Jesus engaged people. He conversed with
Nicodemus, Zacchaeus, the rich young ruler, and the woman
at the well. He could have said, "Look, I'm God and you're not,
so just listen to Me!" But instead, there was give and take in the

conversation. He genuinely cared about them and they could tell. He gave us a model for how we are to share our faith.

Sure, there is a place for "point and counterpoint." We certainly want to be able to defend our beliefs. But know this: no one has ever been argued into the kingdom of God. If they can be argued in, then I suppose they can be argued out. It's possible to win the argument and lose the soul.

Scripture tells us to "Let your speech always be with grace [winsome], seasoned with salt, that you may know how you ought to answer each one" (Col. 4:6). To "win some" you must be winsome. Or to put it another way, be friendly, engaging, and caring.

> But know this: no one has ever been argued into the kingdom of God. If they can be argued in, then I suppose they can be argued out. It's possible to win the argument and lose the soul.

Jesus patiently goes back and forth with the woman at the well. He addresses her questions and gives her clear answers. We need to follow His example. I have seen attempts at evangelism turn into shouting matches. I remember going out and sharing my faith with a brand-new Christian once. I told him to just observe, but I suppose he felt ready after a few weeks of knowing the Lord to dive right in. One particular biker-type dude we encountered was not very responsive to what I was saying about his need for Jesus Christ. My young friend shouted, "Well, the Bible says to not cast your pearls before pigs!" This understandably only escalated an already tense situation, and I excused us from the conversation, trying to explain to my young

Christian friend that his choice was not the best verse to quote at that particular moment. Nor was shouting at someone a good way to win them to Christ.

Considering the size of the man he said it to, it was also a good way to get beat up!

A number of years ago, we were doing an evangelistic crusade in Honolulu at the Aloha Stadium. I was walking down the main drag of Waikiki beach when I came across a man with a placard emblazoned with the words "The wages of sin are death!" This man was shouting at passersby—with some glee I might add—"You are all going to Hell!" I stopped in front of this man and said, "Why don't you put the rest of that passage on the back of your sign and give people some hope? The rest of that verse is, 'But the gift of God is eternal life in Jesus Christ our Lord'" (Rom. 6:23). This guy did not like that one bit and he screamed in my face, "You are going to Hell!" This man was not helping people come to Christ. He was, in my opinion, keeping people from Christ.

A person can say the right thing in the wrong way.

It is true that people who do not know Jesus Christ are going to Hell, but you don't have to be happy about it. The great evangelist D. L. Moody once said that no one should ever talk about Hell to a nonbeliever without a tear in his eye.[7]

If sharing your faith has you screaming in anger at people, you have already lost the battle. Paul wrote to young Timothy, "A servant of the Lord must not quarrel but must be kind to everyone, be able to teach, and be patient with difficult people. Gently instruct those who oppose the truth. Perhaps God will change those people's hearts, and they will learn the truth" (2 Tim. 2:24–25 NLT).

Here is the thing we must understand: the gospel message must be clearly, boldly, verbally, and lovingly stated to the person you are speaking to. Paul writes, "For since, in the wisdom of God, the world through wisdom did not know God, it pleased God through the foolishness of the message preached to save those who believe" (1 Cor. 1:21). You don't have to raise your voice to preach the message, but you must articulate it.

It is important for us to know that when sharing our faith, we do not deal with everyone the same way. It is worth noting that Jesus never dealt with any two people in exactly the same way. There is not a "one size fits all" approach to evangelism.

Everyone is different. The conversation that Jesus had with the woman at the well is markedly different than the one He had with Nicodemus. These two examples are a case study on how to adapt and become, as Paul said, "all things to all men" (1 Cor. 9:22). The apostle Paul wrote, "I have become a slave to all people to bring many to Christ. Yes, I try to find common ground with everyone, doing everything I can to save some" (1 Cor. 9:19, 22 NLT). This does not mean that we compromise or do questionable things. We do not have

> It is true that people who do not know Jesus Christ are going to Hell, but you don't have to be happy about it. The great evangelist D. L. Moody once said that no one should ever talk about Hell to a nonbeliever without a tear in his eye.

to be irreverent to be relevant. We must never lower our standards in order to extend our reach.

> It is important for us to know that when sharing our faith, we do not deal with everyone the same way. It is worth noting that Jesus never dealt with any two people in exactly the same way. There is not a "one size fits all" approach to evangelism.

What Paul is saying is, as much as possible, we should try to find some common ground with the person we are speaking to. Often in evangelism, Christians will find what they disagree about with a person and then argue, instead of starting with what they may agree with. That is why we must listen carefully and pray for wisdom. Jesus calls us to go "fishing for men," and that means that we use different kinds of bait for different kinds of fish.

Nick at Night

Contrast the approach of Jesus in John 4 with His much more direct conversation in John 3 with the spiritual leader Nicodemus. Nicodemus and the woman at the well could not have been more different:

One was a man, the other a woman.
One was moral, the other immoral.
One was highly-educated, the other probably not educated at all.
One was looked up to, the other looked down on.

One was a Jew, the other a Samaritan.

One spoke to Jesus at night, the other in the day.

Yet, despite their differences, one thing was the same for both of them. They both needed Jesus and, to the point, after their conversation with Him, they both believed. The woman believed immediately, and it would appear that Nicodemus believed a bit later. Nicodemus was a well-known, highly respected leader of the Jewish people. Perhaps that is why he came to Jesus at night—because he was afraid to be seen.

He was the man who was supposed to have all the answers, but the fact is, he had many questions. He approached Jesus with great respect, even addressing Him as *Rabbi,* which means "teacher." For a man of Nicodemus's caliber to address Jesus this way was no small praise.

"'Rabbi,' he said, 'we all know that God has sent you to teach us. Your miraculous signs are evidence that God is with you'" (John 3:2 NLT). Jesus effectively cut to the chase with the famous religious leader and said, "I tell you the truth, unless you are born again, you cannot see the Kingdom of God" (John 3:3 NLT). Allow me a loose paraphrase of the words of Jesus: "Buddy, you already know these things; you must be born all over again."

We do not read of him believing immediately after this nighttime conversation with Christ, but we do see him appear later, along with Joseph of Arimathea, claiming the body of Jesus after He was crucified. Some start strong in the Christian life, and then crash and burn later on; Nicodemus had a slow start but a great end. Nicodemus reminds me quite a bit of my father,

Oscar Laurie, whom I talked about in the beginning of this book. Like Nicodemus, Oscar was moral, educated, and searching.

> You may be down and out, or you may be up and out, but you are still out. Jesus says, "Come on in!"

You may be down and out, or you may be up and out, but you are still out. Jesus says, "Come on in!"

Jesus continued His conversation with Nicodemus, but with a much different approach than He took with the woman at the well.

———

"Lord, never let us fall into the trap of thinking it is ever too late. That we have done anything so wrong, that we have said anything so hurtful, that we have sinned so boldly as to miss the opportunity to be known and loved by You. Teach us to not argue with our neighbors, but to love them the way Jesus loved. You've modeled the way; now give us the strength to imitate You. In Jesus' name I pray, Amen."

———

CHAPTER 7

The How-To (The Big One That Got Away)

Then there was the conversation between Jesus and the rich young ruler.

To be a ruler at this time, you had to be at least thirty years old. Yet, we are told he was young, so we can assume this young man was in his early thirties. He had certainly succeeded in life. He was a well-respected spiritual leader and was also quite wealthy. Perhaps he rode in on a gleaming chariot tricked-out with custom wheels and exhaust, or on a beautiful Arabian stallion. Whatever the case, I am sure he made quite an impression wherever he went.

This brash young man came up to Jesus with some opening compliments; then he asked this question of Jesus: "What must I do to inherit eternal life?" (Luke 18:18 NIV). Perhaps he thought

Christ would be impressed with him. But Jesus could see right into this young man's heart, and He could see the obstacle that was keeping him away from God.

In response to his question, Jesus recited a number of commandments to the young man and told him he should obey them. The young man foolishly shot back, "I've obeyed all these commandments since I was young" (Luke 18:21 NLT). Of course, this was simply not true.

Understand why Jesus cited the Commandments in the first place. The Commandments were not given to make us righteous, but to show how unrighteous we are. They were given to open our eyes and shut our mouths (see Rom. 3:19). If this young man had been honest, he would have admitted to breaking the Commandments many times. Instead, he boasted of keeping them.

Then we come to an amazing passage. Right after the young ruler said this, we read, "Looking at the man, Jesus felt genuine love for him" (Mark 10:21 NLT).

There is a lesson for us there: regardless if our listener is responsive to our message or not, we should still show love to him or her.

The fact is, Jesus, being God, was omniscient, which means all-knowing. Jesus knew what was really going on in this young man's heart and called him out, just like He did with the woman at the well. Jesus could see that this young man's sin was breaking the first commandment; the ruler was placing another god before the Lord. And this man's god clearly was his possessions.

That's why Jesus then said, "There is still one thing you haven't done. . . . Go and sell all your possessions and give the money to the poor, and you will have treasure in heaven. Then come, follow me" (Mark 10:21 NLT). This particular statement of Christ has been greatly misunderstood. It is sometimes used to assert that Jesus calls everyone who follows Him to a life of poverty. But Jesus never said anything like this to any other person. It was specifically directed to this rich young ruler.

> There is a lesson for us there: regardless if our listener is responsive to our message or not, we should still show love to him or her.

There were other wealthy men Jesus encountered. Nicodemus, for example, was a wealthy man, and the Lord said nothing of the kind to him. But Jesus said this to this rich young ruler because he was clearly possessed by his possessions. If that were not the case, he would have agreed to this request of Christ. But because those things were his "god," we instead read, "At this the man's face fell, and he went away sad, for he had many possessions" (Mark 10:22 NLT).

I think it's entirely possible that if this rich young ruler would have agreed to Christ's command, Jesus may have then told him to disregard it—like when He tested Abraham by asking him to sacrifice his son Isaac. But we will never know.

Again, the point I am making is that Jesus never dealt with any two people in exactly the same way. Nor should we.

Now back to the woman at the well. This cynical woman is starting to wonder, *Could this be the Messiah?* Her hardened heart is beginning to soften. She sees the love and compassion in His eyes. The same may happen to you as you are speaking with someone. Suddenly "the light goes on" and they are getting it. This is because the Holy Spirit is at work, convicting and convincing a person of their need for Christ, through you. It's like getting a bite on your fishing line.

> Again, the point I am making is that Jesus never dealt with any two people in exactly the same way. Nor should we.

It's at this time we must remember the following: when sharing your faith, keep your eye on the ball. More than one batter has struck out because he did not keep his eye on the ball, and the same could be said about talking to other people about Jesus.

The Big One That Got Away

I don't have many fishing stories to draw on, but one comes to mind. Years ago, I was in Alaska with some friends, Dennis, Lonnie, and Dwight. We went fishing on the Kenai River, which is filled with massive king salmon. Our guide showed us how to use our equipment and we dropped our lines into the water. I asked how we would know if we were getting a bite. The guide told us there would be no question about it because of the size of these fish.

Dennis kept calling out that he had a "hit," but I don't know if a fish ever got close to his hook. Meanwhile, Dwight said nothing; he just patiently waited. Suddenly I got a hit and my whole pole almost went into the water. I firmly grabbed my pole and furiously began to reel this beast in. It was a big one for sure.

I was already seeing a delicious fish dinner on our plates and forming the story of how I got him. I pulled the massive king salmon right up to the boat but the guide was not fast enough to net him, and he broke the line and swam off. The guide said he was at least a fifty-pounder. To say I was disappointed is an understatement. (Now when I talk about it, people roll their eyes and think it's another fish story.) Meanwhile, patient Dwight got a hit, reeled his salmon in, and got the catch of the day.

Sometimes, in sharing our faith, we think we have a person "on the hook," so to speak, and it appears they are going to commit their lives to Christ, and then they break away. But we must never give up.

This woman at the well was trying to "break the line," but Jesus was not to be deterred. As far as she was concerned, by pointing out her sin, Jesus was getting a little too close for comfort. So she did what nonbelievers often do when under the conviction of the Holy Spirit. She changed the subject! She said to Jesus, "Our fathers worshiped on this mountain, and you Jews say that in Jerusalem is the place where one ought to worship" (John 4:20). There was an ongoing debate between Samaritans and Jews about where God was to be worshipped. Jesus could have easily engaged on this. The fact is, the Samaritans had this all wrong.

But Jesus did not labor that point; instead He put it into context with the big picture. Jesus essentially said to her, "Lady, it's not about what kind of building we worship in or even where we worship. God is a Spirit; we must worship Him in spirit and truth" (see John 4:24).

This often happens in a dialogue about the gospel. People come under the conviction of the Holy Spirit and want to get you off message, so they will barrage you with endless questions:

"Why are there so many denominations out there?"
"What about the person who has never heard the gospel; will God send them to Hell?"
"Why is the Bible so full of contradictions?

Or the conversation could be diverted to a heated political discussion. People will try to take you down endless rabbit trails that are secondary at best. I try to address the issue they are asking about, and then come back to the core issue: the gospel.

The main thing is to keep the main thing the main thing. And the "main thing" is *the gospel* faithfully delivered!

Again, Jesus was having a dialogue, not a monologue, with her. This is very important in one-on-one evangelism. You ask questions, and you actually listen to the answers. Then you appropriately apply the gospel to their situation. If I were speaking with a person like this woman, I would appeal to the emptiness in their life and show them how Christ could fill the void. I would clearly mention why the void was there to begin with (because we have all sinned and fallen short of God's glory), and that repentance and belief were required. But if I were speaking with someone who was on their deathbed, I would focus more on eternity. I would ask them a question along the lines of "Are you ready to meet God?"

Going back to the rich young ruler, we see that Jesus often answered a question with a question. The ruler asks Jesus, "Good Teacher, what must I do to inherit eternal life?" Instead of giving this guy the gospel, Jesus responds, "Why do you call me good? . . . Only God is truly good" (Mark 10:17–18 NLT).

> The main thing is to keep the main thing the main thing. And the "main thing" is *the gospel* faithfully delivered!

Why did Jesus take that approach? The Lord was drawing him out and giving him an opportunity to believe. For instance, someone says to you, "Why do you think Jesus was anything more than just a great moral teacher?" You might answer a question with a question: "What makes you think Jesus was a great moral teacher? Have you read His teachings? What do you think is the most important thing He said?" The usual answer would be that they have never read His teachings, and you could point some of them out.

Someone might ask the question, "What about the person who has never heard the gospel? Will God send them to Hell?" This one is usually asked to put you off and hopefully silence you. You could respond, "Why do you ask that? Do you believe in Hell? Do you think anyone deserves to go there? If not, why? Most people would in fact believe that some people should be assigned to Hell—someone like, say, Adolph Hitler. You can answer their question and bring them back to the point, saying something like, "God will judge us according to the light we have received and the truth we've been shown. No one wants a person saved more than Christ Himself. But here's the bottom line: you *have* heard the gospel and you will be held accountable."

There was the time the religious leaders tried to trap Christ with the tax issue. They asked Him the question, "Is it lawful to pay taxes to Caesar or not?" (Matt. 22:17). They were trying to place Jesus on the horns of a dilemma. If He said it was right to pay the taxes that Rome demanded, the people would turn on Him because they were overtaxed. If He said it was not right to pay these taxes, the government would turn on Him, as that would be considered rebellion. Instead, Jesus asked for a Roman coin. Again He answers a question with a question: "Whose image is on this coin?"

"Caesar's!" they reply.

"Then give to Caesar what belongs to Caesar and give to God what belongs to God!" (see Matt. 22:20–21). Talk about turning a situation around.

Coming back to the woman at the well, Jesus knows it's time to go to the next level. Her initial cynicism has given way to curiosity and now it has become belief. "The woman said to Him, 'I know that Messiah is coming. . . . When He comes, He will tell us all things.'

"Jesus said to her, 'I who speak to you am He'" (John 4:25–26). Jesus was effectively saying, "Woman, you are talking to the Messiah right now!"

That was it! She believed on the spot. And that's how long it takes to believe in Jesus Christ. It does not take years, months, or even days. It can happen in a moment—an instant.

"I Don't Want to Talk about It!"

I mentioned how the woman at the well reminds me of my mother. My mom was raised in a Christian home and went to a strong Southern Baptist church every week with her parents and siblings. Her parents insisted she also attend Sunday and Wednesday night services as well. My mother did not like that one bit. She always had a rebellious streak, so to get away from home she married early in life. That marriage quickly ended and then my mom spent the good part of her life on a search. But as time passed, her beauty began to fade. Her years of hard drinking and chain smoking caught up with her and her kidneys began to fail. By the time she hit seventy, she had to get dialysis three times a week and was just miserable.

Whenever I would bring up the subject of faith over the years, my mother's standard response was, "I don't want to talk about that," and she would quickly change the subject. We prayed for her regularly over the years in hopes that this prodigal daughter would come back to her heavenly Father, who desperately missed her.

One day, as I was getting ready to go to my office at church, I felt especially burdened to go see her. I told my wife, Cathe, "I need to go see my mom today and have 'that' conversation about her soul!" Cathe agreed and prayed for me. When I got to my mom's house, she was alone, and I said I wanted to talk about her spiritual life. She shot back her familiar refrain, "I don't want to talk about it!"

I responded, "Today, we are going to talk about it!" My mom was stubborn but her son is even more stubborn, and we had that long-overdue talk about her soul. Thankfully, that conversation ended with her ultimately making a recommitment to follow Jesus Christ. She was in our church the following week. Sadly, she died a month later. I'm so glad I had "that" conversation.

Has the Holy Spirit been nudging you to do the same with someone you know? Don't put it off. You never know how long a person will live, including yourself.

―――――――――

"Lord, show us not only what to say, but how to say it. Grant us patience, a listening ear, discernment, and most of all, give us love for our neighbor. Make us winsome missionaries to everyone we meet, in Jesus' name I pray, Amen."

―――――――――

CHAPTER 8

The Power of Your Personal Story

Now I want to help you discover one of the most effective tools in your evangelistic toolbox: your personal story. It is often called your testimony. Everyone who has put his or her faith in Jesus Christ has a testimony. Granted, some are more dramatic than others, but every story is valid, including yours.

The woman at the well, married and divorced five times, certainly had one. She was what we would call "a woman with a reputation." After her conversation with Jesus, she believed in Him and immediately went out and began to tell others. I'm sure everyone knew her story and they could see the radical transformation that had taken place in her life after her encounter with Jesus Christ. Her testimony was powerful and "many of the Samaritans of that city believed in Him because of the word of the woman who testified, 'He told me all that I ever did'" (John 4:39).

A person can argue all day with you about certain facts. But they cannot argue with your personal story of how you came to faith. Using your testimony as a bridge is very effective because it helps to find that common ground with the person you are speaking with. They may be surprised that you were not always the way that you are now as a Christian—that you did not always believe what you now believe.

You could say something like, "This is the way I used to think and the way I used to view Christians and the church, but then . . ." Fact is, the way you used to think may be the way the person you are speaking with is presently thinking. You are showing them how and why you changed your direction in life—how and why you became a follower of Jesus Christ. Perhaps you struggled with drugs and alcohol. Perhaps you were in a life of crime. You may have been living in immorality. Then again, perhaps you were not addicted to anything, and instead were very successful in your field, but there was still an emptiness in your life.

The main thing is just tell your story. Every testimony is valid because there is someone out there a lot like you.

What's Your Story?

Some might be moved and convinced after hearing of a former criminal who came to Christ, but not everyone would relate to that story. They might even dismiss it, thinking they don't need Christ because only "that kind of person" needs Him but they don't. They need to understand that everyone needs Jesus because everyone has sinned!

Even if you were raised in the church and never went out and tasted all the things this world has to offer, that is still a testimony.

Let me tell you your story without even knowing you.

> The main thing is just tell your story. Every testimony is valid because there is someone out there a lot like you.

- You were in rebellion against God because of your sin.
- You heard the gospel.
- You believed in Jesus and turned from your sin.
- He forgave you of all your sins and gave you a peace and purpose in life.
- Now, instead of going to Hell, you are going to Heaven.

Every one of us can tell our story. You don't have to be an expert in theology to do so. It's worth noting that the apostle Paul often used his personal testimony when he spoke. Though he was a brilliant orator and extremely knowledgeable about Scripture, he often started by telling his own story to build a bridge to his listeners. His message before the Roman leader Agrippa is the perfect example.

After talking about the fact that he had been raised in a strict religious Jewish home and that he felt he was doing God's work when he began to hunt down and arrest Christians, he described what happened to change him:

"One day I was on such a mission to Damascus, armed with the authority and commission of the leading priests. About noon, Your Majesty, as I was on the road, a light from heaven brighter than the sun shone down on me and my companions. We all fell down, and I heard a voice saying to me in Aramaic, 'Saul, Saul, why are you persecuting me? It is useless for you to fight against my will.'

"'Who are you, lord?' I asked.

"And the Lord replied, 'I am Jesus, the one you are persecuting. Now get to your feet! For I have appeared to you to appoint you as my servant and witness. You are to tell the world what you have seen and what I will show you in the future. And I will rescue you from both your own people and the Gentiles.'" (Acts 26:12–17 NLT)

Now that is a dramatic testimony. But then Paul gets to what it really means to be a Christian.

"'Yes, I am sending you to the Gentiles to open their eyes, so they may turn from darkness to light and from the power of Satan to God. Then they will receive forgiveness for their sins and be given a place among God's people, who are set apart by faith in me.'" (Acts 26:17–18 NLT)

This is a perfect template to follow. Tell your story as it unfolded, then transition to the message of what the gospel is.

Here now are a few tips about telling your story the right way.

Don't Glorify or Exaggerate Your Past

Accuracy is really important. So is truthfulness. I have noticed that some people's testimonies get more dramatic with the passing of time. Perhaps they think that will make their story more appealing, but if it is not truthful, that is counterproductive. Just tell the truth about your life and what God did for you.

I heard about a man who was telling a dramatic story of how God delivered him from a life of crime and how he had murdered people but had become a Christian. He was really in demand as a speaker until it was revealed that he made the whole thing up! What a travesty! Do you think God needs your made-up story to reach people? Just tell the truth about your past and your present.

Another problem is making your past sound more appealing than your present. I have heard some Christians, in the name of "giving their testimony," go on and on about all the wild parties and fun they had before their conversion. And when they get to the part when they became a believer, it sounds as though their lives ended. If that is the way you are telling the story of how you came to Christ, you are missing all that God has done for you.

Don't Boast about Your Work, Boast in His

I have heard people, in giving their testimonies, talk about the "great sacrifices" they have made to follow Jesus. *Oh please.* Compared to what Jesus gave up for you, it's nothing! Paul summed up his past and had everything in perfect perspective when he said,

> Yes, all the things I once thought were so important are gone from my life. Compared to the high privilege of knowing Christ Jesus as my master, firsthand, everything I once thought I had going for me is insignificant—dog dung. I've dumped it all in the trash so that I could embrace Christ and be embraced by him. (Phil. 3:8 MSG)

Now that's perspective. Fact is, Paul had a very impressive pedigree in his family line and training under the finest teachers of Israel. But he understood it all meant nothing apart from Christ—dog dung, thrown in the trash!

Do you think you made a great sacrifice to follow Jesus Christ? Think about it for a moment. You gave up an ever-present guilt, a deep emptiness in your life, and a future separated from God, in Hell. Instead, Jesus removed your guilt, filled that void inside, and gave you the certainty of a home in Heaven! You gave up nothing in comparison to what Christ gave up to save your soul. Make sure you emphasize that when sharing your personal story.

It's Not about You; It's about Him!

Our story is the bridge, not the destination. The point of sharing your story is so you can tell His story: His love for humanity, His death on the cross, and His resurrection from the dead. Just give the big picture and sum it up as Paul did when standing before a Roman leader. He said that he had "turned from darkness to light" and from the power of Satan to God, and now he had an eternal reward and inheritance.

We don't want people marveling over our story, but over His—the sacrifice that Jesus made, the price that He paid because of His great love for us. When the woman at the well told her story, she pointed to Jesus, and as a result, "many of the Samaritans of that city believed in Him" (John 4:39). As you tell your story, I pray something similar will happen.

"Lord, conform our stories to Your Story. Make our testimonies a retelling of the gospel. Use everything in my life, not to glorify me, but to glorify Your Son. Thank You for sending a messenger to tell me the gospel story, for changing my story, and for sending me to do the same for others. In Jesus' name I pray, Amen."

CHAPTER 9

What Is the Gospel?

This may be the most important chapter of this book. If we get this wrong, most of what you have read will not be of much help. This is the bottom line. This is the message we are called to bring to people. It's called the gospel.

We throw that word around, but do we really know what it means? As I have already mentioned, the word *gospel* means "good news." When sharing the good news we also must present the bad news. We have all heard those "good news/bad news" jokes. I heard one about two old guys who were wondering if there's baseball in Heaven.

They promised each other that the first to die would somehow let the other one know if there is baseball in Heaven. A week later one of them died. And a week after that, his friend recognized his voice coming from the clouds: "Joe, I've got some good news and some bad news," the disembodied voice reports. "The good news is that there is a baseball team in Heaven. The bad news is that you're pitching on Friday."

That is a joke (and not a very good one at that), but the bad news is that we have all broken God's commandments and we fall short of His standards. The Bible says, "All have sinned and fall short of the glory of God" (Rom. 3:23). Some will protest and say something like, "I think I am a good person. I am not a sinner!" I will remind them that the Bible states, "If we say that we have no sin, we deceive ourselves, and the truth is not in us" (1 John 1:8).

What Is Sin?

Don't assume a person who is not a believer will necessarily know what sin is. Two phrases used that help to explain it are "missing the mark" and "crossing the line," which is what the biblical word *trespass* translates to. The Bible says we are "dead in trespasses and sins" (Eph. 2:1). You have seen those signs in city parks where grass has just been planted that say, "No trespassing." When we break the commandments, it's like we are crossing the "No trespassing" line.

This is where the Ten Commandments can come in and help the person you are speaking with understand what sin is. The Commandments, or the Law, are not given to make us righteous but to show us how far we fall short. Again, the Law is given to open our eyes to our sinfulness and shut our mouths. Speaking of the Law's purpose, Paul reminds us, "Obviously, the law applies to those to whom it was given, for its purpose is to keep people from having excuses, and to show that the entire world is guilty before God" (Rom. 3:19 NLT).

Zig Ziglar once said, "The good news is there is nothing we can do that is bad enough to keep us out of Heaven; the bad news is there is nothing we can do good enough to get us into Heaven."

This is why Jesus quoted the Commandments to the rich young ruler. Not to imply that by keeping these commandments one is made right with God—because no one can keep these commandments. In fact, the only person who has ever kept all of the Commandments perfectly was Jesus Christ. That is why He, and He alone, is uniquely qualified to bridge the gap between sinful humanity and a holy God, whom we have all repeatedly offended through our sin. Jesus lived a perfect life, then He died a perfect death for us on the cross. Jesus quoted the Commandments to the rich young ruler to show how hopeless his condition was, and yet standing before him was the answer: Jesus Christ Himself! But that young man turned away and missed the opportunity of a lifetime.

So, citing the Commandments, I might ask the person I am speaking with, "Have you ever stolen anything? Have you ever taken God's name in vain? Have you ever told a lie?" Most people will admit to this.

But sin also means to "fall short of a mark." And what is the mark, or standard, that God has set for humanity? (Are you sitting down?) Answer: absolute and total perfection. Jesus said, "Be perfect, even as your Father in heaven is perfect" (Matt. 5:48 NLT). A person will usually protest and say to you, "Are you perfect?" And, of course, the answer is no. That is where Jesus comes in.

People will protest and sometimes say, "But I am still a good person!" You might be surprised to hear that I will not necessarily dispute that. I might say, "I'm sure you are in many ways a good person, relatively speaking, but here is the problem: you are not good enough to get to Heaven." Heaven is not for good people; it is for forgiven people. And one sin is enough to keep us out of Heaven, for the Scripture says, "Whoever shall keep the whole law, and yet stumble in one point, he is guilty of all" (James 2:10).

And that brings us to the bottom line of the gospel: It is the death of Jesus Christ on the cross for all sinners, and His resurrection from the dead.

What Is Salvation?

A jeweler will display a sparkling ring or beautiful necklace against black velvet. He does this to display the beauty of the object being presented. God has sought to show us just how good the Good News is by first telling us the bad. Seeing our complete weakness, our inability to do anything to alleviate our miserable condition, God did the ultimate for us. He sent His one and only Son to die for us!

Paul writes, "When we were utterly helpless, Christ came at just the right time and died for us sinners. Now, most people would not be willing to die for an upright person, though someone might perhaps be willing to die for a person who is especially good. But God showed his great love for us by sending Christ to die for us while we were still sinners" (Rom. 5:6–8 NLT).

I love the way Paul personalized it in Galatians 2:20 when he said that the Son of God "loved *me* and gave Himself for *me*"! (italics added). Paul also sums up the essential gospel message in 1 Corinthians 15:3–4: "I passed on to you what was most important and what had also been passed on to me. Christ died for our sins, just as the Scriptures said. He was buried, and he was raised from the dead on the third day, just as the Scriptures said" (NLT).

Jesus gave us the gospel in a nutshell in John 3:16. This is a verse every Christian should commit to memory. Now, there are other elements I will mention, but this is the cornerstone: the death and resurrection of Jesus Christ. Someone once asked the great British preacher C. H. Spurgeon if he could put in a few words his Christian faith. He said that it could be summed up in four words: "Jesus died for me."

Still, we need to have a good working knowledge of how to share the essential gospel message. It seems that we find two extremes when it comes to this topic: we tend to either add to it or take away from it. We add elements that are not essential to the core message, like baptism or good works as essential requirements for salvation. Those are good things, but should come after a person believes. To miss this is to get the cart before the horse.

Overcomplicating it can also be problem. This sometimes happens by using archaic language that a nonbeliever doesn't understand. The audience we largely address today is not like the people gathered on the day of Pentecost, when Peter preached and three thousand believed. These were biblically literate people that understood certain scriptural ideas. Our audience today would be more like the crowd assembled at Mars Hill in Athens, whom Paul spoke to in Acts 17. They were biblically illiterate, more familiar with Greek philosophers and poets. They were a completely secular culture.

The Gospel Is More than an Additive

Another problem in sharing the gospel is we may leave out the complete message. Some will share Jesus as though He were the ultimate "additive'" to one's life to make it better. Loose paraphrase, "If you believe in Jesus, you will have joy and peace and purpose in life. He will give you more 'spring in your step' and make your teeth whiter!"

Now, while it is true Christ will indeed give the person who believes in Him joy, purpose, and peace (I'm not so sure about whiter teeth), it is also true that, in a way, these are more the "fringe benefits" of the faith. For example, a nonbeliever hearing your presentation may say, "I already am a happy person. I don't think I need God in my life. What will happen if I don't believe?"

You might respond by saying, "Well, if you don't believe, you will end up in a very uncomfortable place!" Just as it is wrong to only speak on the benefits of faith, it is also wrong to not warn of the repercussions of rejecting Christ.

The Bottom Line: The most significant thing that happens to us when we turn from our sin and put our faith in Christ is we change our eternal address . . . from Hell to Heaven.

But we are reluctant to use the "h-word," aren't we? We are afraid it will offend our listener.

I am afraid if we don't tell the person the whole truth of the gospel we might offend God!

But to avoid the topic of Hell because it makes us uncomfortable is a huge mistake. Consider that Jesus spent more time talking about Hell than any other preacher in the Bible. That is because He alone has seen it, and He does not want any person created in His image to end up in this horrible place. Granted, it is not easy to broach this subject. Timothy Keller points out, "In our culture, divine judgment is one of Christianity's most offensive doctrines."[8]

At this point, a nonbeliever will usually ask something along the lines of, "But how could a God of love send someone to Hell?"

To start with, Hell was not created for people, but according to Jesus, it was made for "the devil and his angels" (Matt. 25:41). If a person ends up in Hell, God is simply giving them what they wanted. C. S. Lewis said, "There are only two kinds of people in the end: those who say to God, 'Thy will be done,' and those to whom God says, in the end, '*Thy* will be done.' All that are in Hell choose it, and without that self-choice, there could be no Hell."[9]

- To promise Heaven and not warn of Hell is to offer forgiveness without repentance.
- To preach the gospel without the cross is a false message giving false hope.
- If we really love people, we need to tell the truth about eternity.

That's doesn't mean we become *"hellfire and brimstone preachers."* What it does mean is we do not hold back if they reject God's offer. Let them know what the consequences are. Jude 22–23 says, "Show mercy to those whose faith is wavering. Rescue others by snatching them from the flames of judgment" (NLT).

Speak Their Language

In Paul's time, Athens was the cultural and intellectual center of the world. It was the base of the great philosophers Socrates, Plato, Aristotle, and many others. Almost all philosophies follow, to some degree, the teachings of these very men. There were two primary groups that Paul was addressing in Athens: Epicureans and Stoics.

Epicureans believed in the pursuit of pleasure. They did not believe that there was any order to the universe, so we might as well just live for the moment. The Stoics were more disciplined, with an almost Buddhist-like worldview.

What is the culture we are called to speak to? According to *USA Today*, the newest group we are addressing are the "Nones." The article states, "For decades, if not centuries, America's top religious brand has been 'Protestant.' No more. . . . Where did they go? Nowhere, actually. They didn't switch to a new religious brand, they just let go of any faith affiliation or label. . . . This group, called 'Nones,' is now the nation's second-largest category only to Catholics, and outnumbers the top Protestant denomination, the Southern Baptists."[10]

What do the Nones believe? Answer: Nothing in particular, but they are open to spirituality. One was quoted to say that she was once a Christian, but "let go of her belief." She said, "There is so much I cannot prove. Instead of saying 'I believe,' I say 'Maybe' and 'Who knows?'"

A related article points out that Nones believe in astrology and reincarnation and 58 percent say they feel "a deep connection" with nature and the earth.[11] As you can see, "there is nothing new under the sun." Malcolm Muggeridge said, "All new news is old news happening to new people."[12]

So, how do we reach a culture that thinks like this? The same way the first-century believers reached their culture: with the powerful message of the gospel.

This is why Paul said, "I am not ashamed of the gospel of Christ, for it is the power of God to salvation for everyone who believes, for the Jew first and also for the Greek" (Rom. 1:16). Whether I stand behind the pulpit at an evangelistic event before thousands, or speak to an individual, I have complete confidence in my message. I don't have to add to it or make it "more appealing." I just need to proclaim it and watch God work.

My objective is to simply "let the lion out of the cage."

This is why Paul called the gospel "the power of God." The Greek word Paul uses that translates to "power" is an

> So, how do we reach a culture that thinks like this? The same way the first-century believers reached their culture: with the powerful message of the gospel.

interesting word. It is *dunamis*. This word entered the English language when Alfred Nobel made the discovery that would become his fortune. He discovered a power stronger than anything the world had known up to that time. He asked a friend who was a Greek scholar what the word for "explosive power" was. His friend answered, "*Dunamis!*" Nobel said, "Well, I'm going to call my discovery by the same name!" So Nobel called his explosive power "dynamite." Paul is telling us that there is explosive power in the essential gospel message.

There in "Idol Central," the city of Athens, Paul walked about and took it all in. One of the ancient writers tells us that at this time there were thirty thousand gods in Athens!

Paul assessed the situation and adapted accordingly. We must do the same today, starting with speaking in a language that people understand. So often as Christians, we are out of touch with the people we are speaking to.

Perhaps this is due in part to having submerged ourselves into a Christian subculture. For instance, if you were to approach a nonbeliever cold and ask, "Excuse me, but are you washed in the blood?" they might think you are crazy! As believers, we understand that you are speaking of being cleansed by confessing your sin and being washed in the blood of Christ.

Or you might say to a person who is not yet a Christian, "Are you a part of the body of Christ? If so, you should not 'walk in the flesh'"! Now you sound as though you just landed from another planet! Washed in blood, part of a body, but not in the flesh? Can you see how that would not make sense to a nonbeliever who has no knowledge whatsoever of the gospel, or the Bible in general? These are not terms they know or understand.

I am not suggesting you do not use biblical terminology when sharing your faith. I am simply saying you must not expect that the average "garden-variety" non-believer would necessarily know what you are talking about. Having said that, I do believe we want to quote and use Scripture in our evangelism.

That does not mean you have to carry a massive black Bible with gleaming gold pages with you wherever you go (or a custom-designed one with Popsicle sticks). You can carry a Bible in your backpack, briefcase, or purse, but the best place to hide God's Word is in your heart. When you quote Scripture, you do not have to shout it or quote it in an "otherworldly" way. You can, in a very conversational manner, share the Word of God.

> Paul assessed the situation and adapted accordingly. We must do the same today, starting with speaking in a language that people understand. So often as Christians, we are out of touch with the people we are speaking to.

Why do this? Because there is power in God's Word. *My* word can return void, and so can yours, but *God's Word* never will. God compares His Word to supernatural seed that goes into the soil of the human heart. God says of His Word, "I send it out, and it always produces fruit. It will accomplish all I want it to, and it will prosper everywhere I send it" (Isa. 55:11 NLT).

Speaking of the power of Scripture, Paul says, "All Scripture is inspired by God and is useful to teach us what is true and to make us realize what is wrong in our lives. It corrects us when we are wrong and teaches us to do what is right. God uses it to prepare and equip his people to do every good work" (2 Tim. 3:16–17 NLT).

—————

"Lord, give us clarity about what the gospel is, so that we can clearly explain it to others. Help us not to oversimplify the gospel, and short-change our hearers. Help us not to overcomplicate the gospel, and confuse our hearers. Send your Spirit to drive out the author of confusion, so that more might know Your Son! In Jesus' name I pray, Amen."

—————

CHAPTER 10

Closing the Deal

I was a newly minted Christian, very excited about my newfound faith, and had already led a couple of people to the Lord. Though only a few weeks old spiritually, I felt I was ready for just about anything, and that, of course, was not true. I had not really been grounded in my theology yet and needed to study Scripture more to deal with those oft-asked questions that nonbelievers have. That's when I saw my old buddy, Gregg.

We had pretty much grown up together and we both had an artistic flair. We had collected reptiles in our younger years as kids and also, I am sorry to say, in our late teen years did drugs together as well. I had not seen Gregg since the encounter at my friend's house with my Popsicle-cross Bible. After that episode, I personally told Gregg that he did not need to worry about me becoming too fanatical as a Christian. "You will never see Greg Laurie walking around carrying a Bible with a cross hanging around his neck saying, 'Praise the Lord!'" Gregg seemed reassured by my confident statement.

Now, fast-forward a couple of months. I'm seventeen years old and I'm walking down the street in Newport Beach and I see Gregg walking toward me. As I approach him I see concern in his eyes, for there I am carrying my Bible, a cross around my neck, and before I could catch myself, I blurted out, "Praise the Lord!" We both stopped and just started laughing. We had known each other a long time.

"Gregg, I know this looks strange, but I have to tell you that Christ has so changed my life I just have to go out and tell people!" Gregg seemed intrigued. I continued talking about the changes that had happened in my life and the newfound peace and joy I was now experiencing, and my old friend was drinking it all in.

What if Gregg accepted Christ? I thought as I shared more. Suddenly, and seemingly out of nowhere, some older guy in his twenties interrupted our conversation. He was the owner of what we then called "a head shop" which consisted of drug paraphernalia, posters, black lights, and other things people who get high like. "I have a few questions for you, Christian!" he said with an evil look in his eye and a smirk on his face.

"Fire away!" I confidently said, feeling I was ready for whatever. I cannot recall what his questions were specifically, but they came in rapid succession, each one a bit harder to respond to than the last. I was completely overwhelmed.

"Yeah, what about those questions, Laurie?" Gregg chimed in. I sheepishly responded, "I don't know," and they both had a hearty laugh at my expense. I walked away from that encounter humbled and ashamed. I felt like a complete failure.

I remember praying and asking God to help me study and prepare more. I immersed myself in apologetics so I would be prepared the next time around. Scripture tells us that we should "always be ready to give a defense to everyone who asks you a reason for the hope that is in you" (1 Pet. 3:15). The word for "defense" in the Greek is *apologia*, which means "a legal defense for our faith, as in a court of law."

Every Christian who wants to lead others to Christ needs to have at least a basic understanding of their faith and how to answer difficult and oft-asked questions. We need, to the best of our ability, to try to answer the difficult questions people ask and then pivot back to our main objective: Jesus Christ and Him crucified.

> Every Christian who wants to lead others to Christ needs to have at least a basic understanding of their faith and how to answer difficult and oft-asked questions.

Popping the Question

This is where it falls apart for most Christians: closing the deal, or pulling in the net. How do we make that transition from sharing our testimony and the essential gospel message to actually leading another person to Christ? It's not as hard as you may think. But you have to ask the question sooner or later of the person you are speaking to: "Would you like to ask Jesus Christ into your heart right now?"

It's somewhat like a marriage proposal. I have read stories of some pretty dramatic proposals, including a friend of mine who went diving with his girlfriend and wrote his proposal on an underwater tablet for her to read: "Will you marry me?"

My wife, Cathe, tells me that I never properly proposed to her. I could not remember, so I will have to go with her version of this story. She says we were out having dinner, and I rather matter-of-factly said, "Well, I guess we're getting married, huh?" What a romantic I was! Thankfully, she looked past my lack of a proper proposal and agreed anyway.

But there is that same tension when we are thinking of asking the nonbeliever we are speaking to if they would like to ask Jesus into their life. Frankly, I think we overcomplicate this. I vividly remember the first time I was able to lead someone to Christ.

I was only weeks old in my faith at that point, and I was again down at the beach in Newport looking for people to engage with the gospel. I was armed with a copy of a little evangelistic tract that outlined the gospel message. I had not even memorized its contents yet. But the pastor had told us to go share our faith and that was exactly what I was going to do.

Seeing a woman sitting on the beach who was around the age of my mother, I decided I would talk to her. Perhaps she would take pity on a nervous teenager. "Excuse me?" I said, my voice trembling from nerves. "I was wondering if I could talk to you about Jesus Christ!" She agreed and I sat down and simply opened up that little evangelistic booklet and started reading verbatim.

"The Four Spiritual Laws," I began, reading the title. As I took her through each point, I was thinking to myself, *This is not going to work. She will never want to ask Jesus Christ to come into her life after such a shoddy presentation as this!* I began to rush so I could just get the whole thing over with, vowing to not try this again. Then I came across a question in the little booklet. "Is there any reason why you should not accept Jesus Christ into your life?" I read aloud, rather robotically, expecting no response on her part.

I realized after I read it that I should look up at her, as I had just asked her a very important question. She said, "No!"

Suddenly, I was jarred to reality. "Are you saying *you want to accept Jesus Christ* into your life right now?" I said with some disbelief. "Yes, I do!" she said.

I suddenly panicked. *What do I do now?* I thought to myself. In the most reverent tone I could muster, I said, "Let's bow our heads and pray." (I had seen the pastor do that at church.) She closed her eyes and I frantically searched that little booklet for some clue as to what to do next, when I came across a suggested prayer a person could pray who wanted to become a follower of Jesus.

"Then just pray this prayer after me," I said. And she did. Even as I was leading her in that prewritten prayer, I was thinking, *This will never work! There is no way she is really coming to Jesus right now after a poor presentation like that.* At this point, the prayer was done.

We both opened our eyes and she smiled and said, "Something just happened to me!"

Indeed. Something had just happened to me too. I discovered how easy it could be to lead another person to Christ.

I am not suggesting everyone, or even most people, will respond this way, but I am saying that some will, and more than you may think.

So, when you get to this point, there is no harm in asking the person you are speaking with, "Would you like to ask Jesus Christ into your life right now?" Worst-case scenario: they say no. But what if they say *yes*?

By the way, I never pressure a person to believe. Our job is proclamation, not manipulation.

> So, when you get to this point, there is no harm in asking the person you are speaking with, "Would you like to ask Jesus Christ into your life right now?" Worst-case scenario: they say no. But what if they say *yes*?

A Common Struggle

There seems to be a struggle for many people in this particular area of "closing the deal." I have even seen pastors give outstanding messages in their churches, but when it comes to extending an invitation to accept Christ, it is not clear to the people who want to respond. I invite people to Christ as I feel directed by the Holy Spirit. I will say something like, "Would you like to ask Jesus Christ to come into your life right now?" People usually seem surprised by a question like that and will often respond by saying, "You mean right now? Here?"

"Yes, I do" will be my general response. If you can get away to a private place, that is a good thing, but at the same time, you can pray with them wherever you are. I have done this on the beach, in a parking lot, in a mall, a car, pretty much wherever. I feel very strongly that if a person says they want to commit their lives to Christ, it should be acted on immediately.

I was at lunch the other day with some of the pastors from our church in our favorite seafood restaurant. There is a server there that usually waits on us, and we joked a bit and placed our order. She came back to us with a serious look on her face and said, "I have to ask you a serious question."

I responded, "Go ahead."

She said, "When are your service times at your church?"

We told her and then she said, "I want to come to church this Sunday and rededicate my life to the Lord."

I think my response surprised her. "No," I said. "You need to commit yourself to the Lord right here, right now!"

She hesitated. "Here?" she asked.

Smiling, I said, "Right here, right now."

She agreed and I led her in a prayer of recommitment.

It seemed only fitting in a restaurant that specializes in serving fresh fish that we not let this one get away as we went "fishing for men."

After we prayed, she said, "I feel so much better!"

"Now come to church this Sunday as a newly committed Christian. I'll see you there!" I responded.

Not long ago I read the story of a fisherman who was testing an outboard propeller on a lake in Ohio a number of years ago.

There, in a cove, he saw a giant muskellunge fish lurking near the surface. The fisherman motored toward it and cast unsuccessfully several times before the fish disappeared. A half hour later he returned to the cove where he first spotted the big muskie. It was back!

The fisherman turned on the electric trolling motor and headed toward the beast. As he crept closer, the massive fish suddenly started swimming toward the boat. The fisherman quickly put on a leather glove and plunged his arm into the water, grabbing the fish behind the gills. The fish started thrashing and twisting. The fisherman was having trouble lifting the huge muskie into the boat. Fortunately, a nearby fisherman came over to help, and they were able to wrestle the monster into the fisherman's boat.

The muskellunge weighed more than fifty-three pounds. If he had used a rod and reel, it probably would have broken the record for the biggest muskie ever caught in Ohio. When asked about his fish, the man said, "I was at the right place at the right time, and I was fool enough to grab it."

That's the same attitude we should have in "fishing for men." Being at the right place at the right time, and being "fool enough" to take a risk, and share the gospel! This is where you can lead a person in what is sometimes called the "sinner's prayer."

There is not a specific prayer in Scripture that we can lead them in so I suggest something along the lines of the following. I will usually ask them to pray it out loud after me.

Lord Jesus, I know that I am a sinner. But I also know that You are the Savior. Forgive me of my sins. I repent of them now, and I choose to follow You from this moment forward as my Savior and Lord, my God and Friend. Thank You for dying on the cross for me and rising again from the dead. I ask You to come into my life. I choose to follow You from this day forward. Thank You for loving me and calling me and accepting me. In Jesus' name I pray, Amen.

Now What?

So, let's say God has graciously allowed you to lead a person to Christ. Is that the end of it? No, actually that is the beginning! Now it is your privilege to disciple them. But what does that mean exactly?

Let's go back to the Great Commission again. Jesus said, "Go therefore and make disciples of all the nations, baptizing them in the name of the Father and of the Son and of the Holy Spirit, teaching them to observe all things that I have commanded you; and lo, I am with you always, even to the end of the age" (Matt. 28:19–20).

Note that phrase, "teaching them to observe all things that I have commanded you." Now, your job is to take them under your wing and help them to acclimate to their new commitment to follow Christ. You do not need to be a Bible scholar to do this. In fact, in many ways, you just need to be a friend. You need to model what a follower of Jesus Christ looks like in the real world. You want to help them grow up spiritually.

It could be compared to having a newborn baby or small child around. Children are fickle. A child can go from laughing to crying in a millisecond (sometimes doing both at once!). They can go from total happiness to complete misery.

The young believer can be very vulnerable as well. They need an older believer to stabilize them and ground them in their faith.

I have been the editor of two Bibles that are excellent to use to spiritually ground new believers. They are full of notes I wrote that explain passages but also have tracks that you can follow with the new convert to help them understand basic Bible doctrines. They are *The New Believer's Bible* (Tyndale) and *Start! The Bible for New Believers* (Thomas Nelson). I would highly recommend that you get one of these and go through them with the new believer. I have not only written the notes for these, but I have also used them with new believers and they work very effectively.

My Friend Mark

I already told you how I made a clean break from my old friends after my commitment to Christ. The only Christians I knew were on my high school campus, and I went to a couple of meetings where they had a guest speaker that I did not care much for, so I decided that I would do this whole Christianity thing "solo." Clearly that would not have worked, and that is where a young man who went to my school named Mark came in.

He walked up to me and told me he had seen me go forward at the invitation on our high school campus and prayed to receive Christ into my life. I rather defensively said, "Yeah, so?" He then said that he wanted me to go to his church. I politely refused, saying I really didn't want to. But Mark was persistent! He would not take no for an answer.

In a friendly but direct way he made his case and I finally agreed, albeit it reluctantly. He picked me up at my house and took me to a church that was exploding in growth called Calvary Chapel in Costa Mesa, California. It was in the throes of the Jesus Movement and there were wall-to-wall people.

Not being raised in an affectionate family, I was immediately put off when some girl, seeing me walk in, came and hugged me saying, "Welcome, brother." Honestly, I wanted to leave right there. I was actually relieved to see that every seat was taken so that I would have to sit way in the back. But someone in the front row recognized me from school and gestured for me to join them in the front row! I was not happy about it, but I went and sat next to them.

You see, the problem was, there was just too much love and joy in that place and I was not fully committed yet. But as I listened to the heartfelt worship and heard my first official Bible study from Chuck Smith, the senior pastor, by the end of the service I was hooked. You could not keep me away from the place.

Mark introduced me to other Christians he knew and invited me over to his home for dinner. There was something there I had never seen before: an intact, functioning family—father, mother, and children. After a delicious home-cooked meal, we opened our Bibles and they started telling me great stories from Scripture. I had never heard such wonderful things before and I had so many questions, which they patiently answered for me.

That was discipleship at its very best.

Certainly, you can do that for someone else. As I have already pointed out, not only does this stabilize the new believer, but it can also revive you personally. Sometimes as Christians we can start to take certain truths for granted. It is only when we see someone else discover them for the first time that we "rediscover" them ourselves.

You Can't Love a Man and Hate His Wife

I cannot emphasize enough how important it is to integrate these new believers into your local church. Jesus only started one organization when He walked this earth, and that was the church. Jesus loves the church, and so should we.

If you want to get on my bad side, say something insulting about my wife. In the same way, Jesus loves His bride, the church, and "gave Himself for her."

The church is like an oasis of hope in a desert of hopelessness. You simply cannot grow spiritually without being an active member and participant in a local church.

In the epistle to the Ephesians, Paul talks about how God gave us apostles, prophets, pastors, teachers, and evangelists to help us all to grow up spiritually. Every new believer needs a pastor. For that matter, every mature believer needs a pastor too.

The apostle Paul was not always the great preacher and author of New Testament epistles. His old life as the feared "Saul of Tarsus" was the stuff of legend. Saul was more than an opponent of the Christian faith before his conversion. He was a "Christian-killer." He hunted down followers of Jesus Christ and hauled them away in chains. Saul presided over the death of the courageous young Stephen, who became the first martyr of the church. I can pretty much guarantee that Saul never intended on converting to the Christian

> The church is like an oasis of hope in a desert of hopelessness. You simply cannot grow spiritually without being an active member and participant in a local church.

faith, much less becoming one of its greatest leaders.

So when Jesus confronted Saul on the road to Damascus and Saul was blinded by a brilliant light, he had no idea what was happening. Then he heard those powerful and ominous words, "Saul, Saul, why are you persecuting Me?" (Acts 9:4).

Saul, knowing he was encountering the living God, was terrified. "Who are you?" he asked. I wonder if in his heart of hearts he was saying, "Please don't say you are Jesus!" Then came the powerful reply, "*I am Jesus,* whom you are persecuting!" (v. 5, italics added). Notice how Jesus identifies with the church in this statement. To persecute the church was to persecute Christ Himself.

Saul believed on the spot, saying, "Lord, what do You want me to do?" (v. 6). Saul was instructed to go to the city and further information would come.

Now, here was the problem: Who would ever believe that the feared Saul of Tarsus was now a bona fide follower of Jesus Christ? Answer: pretty much no one.

Enter a very significant individual: Ananias. The Lord spoke to Ananias and told him to go seek out Saul, who was now a believer. God even gave him the address. Ananias was having a very hard time wrapping his mind around the fact that Saul of Tarsus was now a follower of Jesus Christ, and he pushed back. But God said to him, "Go, for he is praying!" This would be like a Jew who was hiding from the Nazis hearing that Adolph Hitler had been saved!

In *The Message* translation, the dialogue between Ananias and the Lord is as follows:

> Ananias protested, "Master, you can't be serious.
> Everybody's talking about this man and the terrible
> things he's been doing, his reign of terror against
> your people in Jerusalem! And now he's shown up
> here with papers from the Chief Priest that give him
> license to do the same to us." But the Master said,
> "Don't argue. Go!" (Acts 9:13–15)

To Ananias's eternal credit, he obeyed the Lord and sought out Saul and prayed for him and assured him. What would have happened to Saul without Ananias? Saul needed a friend, just like every new believer does.

Ananias was truly an "unsung hero" of the Christian faith. He never preached any sermons that we know of. He never had miracles performed by his hand. He never wrote an epistle. But he did reach one who did all of that and more.

Chuck Swindoll, in his book on the apostle Paul from his series *Great Lives from God's Word*, said, "Ananias has been called one of the forgotten heroes of the faith. Indeed he is. There are countless numbers of them serving Christ behind the scenes the world over. Most we will never meet, we'll never know by name. They are content to remain in the shadows, oblivious to the lure of lights and applause. Nevertheless, they are heroes."[13]

The problem for Saul was that some Christians were having a hard time believing he was really converted. We actually read, "When Saul arrived in Jerusalem, he tried to meet with the believers, but they were all afraid of him. They did not believe he had truly become a believer!" (Acts 9:26 NLT).

Enter the second man to play a key role in discipling the newly converted Paul: Barnabas. He put his own credibility on the line and personally vouched for Paul, assuring the believers that Paul really had met Jesus Christ and now was His follower (see Acts 9:27). The very name Barnabas means "son of encouragement." Would you be a Barnabas to a new believer?

If we had more Ananiases and Barnabases, we would have more Pauls. You may not be the next Billy Graham, but you may be the person who nurtures and encourages the next Billy Graham.

===========

*"Lord, equip us with the knowledge of Your Word
and the people You created to effectively share
Your story. Give us a love for Your bride, the church.
Make us into Ananiases and Barnabases; make some
of us into Pauls. Conform us into the image of
Your Son. In Jesus' name I pray, Amen."*

===========

My First "Sermon"

Prior to becoming a Christian, my focus was on becoming a graphic artist, and specifically a cartoonist. As a young man, I corresponded with the legendary Charles Schulz, the creator of *Peanuts,* who graciously answered my barrage of letters filled with questions on how to do what he did.

When I became a believer, there were no evangelistic booklets or tracts that I really liked giving out, especially the illustrated ones, which always seemed to focus on hellfire. My high school art teacher gave us the assignment to illustrate a comic book, which was the easiest thing for me. But then I had a thought: What about a Christian comic, and more the point, one that presented the gospel message?

I had just heard the pastor speak on the story of the woman at the well in John chapter 4, so I gave the little comic the title "Living Water." I turned it in for the class, but then I wondered if it could not have a wider audience. So I took my drawings to that pastor who spoke, Chuck Smith of Calvary Chapel of Costa

Mesa, and he looked it over with a big smile on his face. Chuck told me to redraw it in a format that could be printed, which I did, and for the first press run, thousands were produced. They quickly ran out of stock, so the next order was for ten thousand and those were given out. Then one hundred thousand, and off they went. When it was all said and done, at least a million of them were distributed—perhaps more.

I met people who came to Christ after reading them, as the tracts came complete with a prayer for a nonbeliever to pray. I was delighted that I could use this gift of illustrating to reach people, but I found that I enjoyed engaging people personally with the gospel more than sitting behind a drawing board. But I never envisioned myself as someone who would ever preach. God had different ideas, however.

My Baptism of Fire and Water

Our church would hold mass baptisms at Corona Del Mar Beach, at a little spot that was just perfect, called Pirate's Cove. It was a natural amphitheater and people would gather on the rocky overlook above and watch their friends and family members be baptized in the clear, blue waters of the Pacific. I myself was baptized in this spot and loved to attend these events that would draw up to one thousand people per baptism. The Jesus Movement, a genuine American revival, was in full swing, and these baptisms were featured on the covers of news magazines around the world.

Corona Del Mar was a familiar beach; I used to go there as a kid in high school. I remember waiting in line at the snack bar in the warm summer sun one day, when I heard a man dressed head to toe in black, with a wide-brimmed hat to match, preaching to anyone who would listen. I stood there in my board shorts and T-shirt watching him scream and sweat, and I thought to myself, *Why would anyone do this?* I could have never imagined at this very beach I would soon be called by the Lord to effectively do the same thing.

So, I arrived one day for the baptism, but I had my times wrong and had missed it altogether. Disappointed, I walked along the beach to see if any of my friends were around, when I came upon a small group of Christians who were sitting in a circle, singing some of the songs we sang at church. Taking my place among them, I sang along and noticed there was no real leader. I had read something that morning from Scripture and, after one of the songs ended, I began with quivering voice to share what I felt God had placed on my heart. After I was done, I was relieved and shot up a quick prayer of thanks to the Lord for opening that little door of opportunity.

But the Lord was just getting started.

I have found that He tends to lead us one step at a time. If we take the first step of obedience, He will then show us what the next step is.

I was always reticent when it came to speaking publicly, so this took a lot for me to do. Apparently, I am not alone in this. When people are surveyed and asked what their greatest fears are, public speaking is almost always in the top three, along with the fear of death and flying. I have even seen the fear of speaking publicly listed higher than the fear of dying! That always struck me as a bit extreme: "You have a choice here. You can die or say a few words." And the person says, "Kill me now!"

I had not noticed, but while I gave my "mini-sermon," a couple of girls had joined us. Assuming I was the leader, since I had briefly spoken, they asked one of the Christians in the circle if I might baptize them. Someone leaned over to me and said, "Pastor, could you baptize these girls?" I nearly jumped out of my skin.

"Pastor? Me?" I quickly corrected the person and told them I was not a pastor. But they persisted; would I baptize these girls? I sensed the Lord speaking to me and telling me to do it. So I confidently announced to the group, "These two girls want to be baptized, so let's go over to Pirate's Cove!" We all stood up and began to walk over, and now with about thirty people in tow, I thought, *What on earth am I doing here?*

But I couldn't back out now. We arrived at our destination and I took the two girls out into the water, while the other believers stood on shore watching. It suddenly dawned on me that I had never really observed the technique of baptizing a person. I could not remember exactly what should be done. I fumbled my way through it, baptizing them in the name of the Father, Son, and Holy Spirit. That part I remembered.

I was feeling quite euphoric at this point, saying to the Lord, "Father, thank You for this wonderful opportunity! I'm so glad I responded to Your prompting!"

But the Lord had even more in mind for me on that sunny Southern California day.

Tell Someone!

I noticed that a small crowd had gathered up on the rocks and were watching all of this. As clear as day, God spoke to my heart and said, "Preach the gospel!" This is what I had always feared when I started sharing my faith: that the Lord would nudge me to do this. I simply was not interested. My mind raced back to the sweating preacher, dressed head to toe in black, whom I had seen as a boy on this very beach, and how I never wanted to be that guy. And now . . . I was.

At the same time, I had a boldness and power I had never known before—a power equal to the task. So for the first time in my life, I voluntarily began to speak. I don't recall exactly what I said, but it was something along the lines of, "Maybe you are wondering what we are doing down here, baptizing these people. These girls have put their faith in Jesus Christ, who died on the cross for your sin . . ."

This was not as hard as I thought it would be. In fact, I was even enjoying it. What happened next surprised even me. Without missing a beat, raising my voice a bit louder so as to be heard, I said to the people watching, "If you would like to ask Jesus Christ to come into your life, come down to this beach here and I will pray with you and baptize you too!" It's almost as though I stepped outside of myself for a moment and said, *Greg, what on earth do you think you are doing? You are not a preacher. What, do you think you're Billy Graham?*

All these thoughts rushed through my mind as I was wrapping up my little evangelistic talk. And sure enough, people came—down the stairs, right to where I was standing. I prayed with a couple more people to accept Christ and proceeded to baptize them as well. What a day!

The whole day was like a sneak preview of things to happen later in my life. In time, I would be a pastor and an evangelist, speaking in arenas and stadiums and calling people to Christ, just like Billy Graham did. This was not to happen for a few more years, but I knew now there was no turning back. In many ways, that particular day was a prototype of what I have spent the last forty years of my life doing: teaching the Bible as I did with the group on the beach and preaching the gospel as I did at Pirate's Cove.

I only tell this story to give you a heads-up about what may be in your future if you start telling others about your faith in Jesus Christ. You may not necessarily be teaching Bible studies and preaching and baptizing people. That is a calling that must come from the Lord. But I believe you will find yourself—dare I say it?—"addicted" to serving God. You will find the joy and happiness of serving others and helping them come to and grow in their faith in Christ.

Hopefully you have discovered that sharing your faith is not an option for us as followers of Jesus Christ. The Lord has commanded us to "Go into all the world and preach the gospel." In other words, He has told us to *Tell Someone*. And each of us has a strategic part to play.

Some sow the seed of the gospel, others water the seed others have sown, and even others reap where people have already sown and watered.

The apostle Paul, writing to the believers in the city of Corinth said, "Who then is Paul, and who is Apollos, but ministers through whom you believed, as the Lord gave to each one? I planted, Apollos watered, but God gave the increase" (1 Cor. 3:5–6).

That's right, God gives the increase.

The Lord does not hold us responsible for how many have come to Him through our sharing.

That's His job, not ours.

We are called to faithfulness.

In that final day, Jesus will not say, "Well done, good and successful servant" but rather "good and *faithful* servant" (Matt. 25:23).

We are to be faithful to share this message and leave the results in the hands of God.

After Paul preached on one occasion, we read: "When the Gentiles heard this, they were glad and honored the word of the Lord; and all who were appointed for eternal life believed" (Acts 13:48 NIV).

Yes, I believe that God appoints or chooses us before we choose Him. This is clearly taught in Scripture. Jesus said, "You did not choose me, but I chose you" (John 15:16). But we don't know how that is done. All we know is we have our marching orders from Christ to call all people to Him as we go into "all the world" saying to people, "Let anyone who is thirsty come" (Rev. 22:17 NLT).

The evangelist D. L. Moody once said, "Lord, save the elect and then elect some more!"

A Failure that Turned Out to Be a Success

George Smith thought his ministry was a failure. He felt called to Africa, but he was only there for a short time as a missionary when he was driven from the country. He left behind one convert, a woman. Not long after that, George Smith died on his knees, praying for Africa.

Some years later, a group of men stumbled onto the place in Africa where George Smith had ministered. They found a copy of the Scriptures he had left behind, and they met the one convert of his ministry, who led them to the Lord. Later a missions organization did a study and determined that one hundred years after George Smith left Africa, thirteen thousand people had come to faith through his ministry as one person reached another, who reached another, and so on.

The Bible calls Noah "a preacher of righteousness" (see 2 Pet. 2:5), yet he lived for 120 years without ever seeing a single convert. He stands as an example of all those faithful witnesses out there who don't see a lot of results.

Are you one of those people? Maybe you have been talking to your family for years, and not one has come to believe in Jesus. Maybe you have shared your faith with your neighbors and coworkers but have never had anyone believe as a result of your testimony. You feel that you're the worst evangelist of all time.

But it isn't over until it's over. Your job is to be faithful. Your job is to do your part and leave the results in the hands of God. When we stand before the Lord one day, it isn't going to be about quantity; it is going to be about why and if you were faithful to do what the Lord set before you to do.

You cannot lead everyone to Christ, but by God's grace you can lead someone to Him. I heard it once said "I am only one, but I am one."

- I cannot do everything, but I can do something.
- What I can do, I ought to do.
- And what I ought to do by the grace of God, I WILL DO!

We must all do what we can while we can.

Again, Jesus has told us to "Go into all the world and preach the gospel."

Let's start with the ones we come into contact with today.

Let's do what we can while we can.

Let's get busy, and *Tell Someone*!

Five Steps to Start and Keep an Evangelistic Culture

A note to pastors, teachers, Bible study leaders, and Sunday school teachers on how to have an evangelistic culture in your church.

An evangelistic crusade or outreach is like a "shot in the arm," a catalyst to rally the troops, a call to battle. But the ongoing work of evangelism happens in churches. In fact, what's needed in our churches today is an evangelistic culture.

This is not something that happens naturally; it happens supernaturally. Things always default to mediocrity—never to quality. That's true of businesses, restaurants, stores, and even the church. If you see quality, and life, and an evangelistic culture, it is there because of effort.

And that effort starts with you as the pastor or ministry leader. You cannot take people any further than you yourself have gone. As Paul told Timothy, the farmer that labors must first be a partaker of the fruit (see 2 Tim. 2:6).

How Can You Have an Evangelistic Culture in Your Church?

1. Begin in the Pulpit

If there is a mist in the pulpit, there will be a fog in the pews. I quoted C. H. Spurgeon earlier in this book, but I think his words bear repeating: "The Holy Spirit will move them by first moving you. If you can rest without their being saved, they will rest too. But if you are filled with an agony for them, if you cannot bear that they should be lost, you will soon find that they are uneasy too. I hope you will get into such a state that you will dream about your child or your hearer perishing for lack of Christ, and start up at once and begin to cry, 'O God, give me converts or I die!' Then you will have converts."[14]

2. Articulate the Gospel

You might say, "But I'm a pastor, not an evangelist!" That may be true, but Paul told Timothy to "do the work of an evangelist" (2 Tim. 4:5). You need to specifically break down the gospel and explain it to people. Try to imagine that you are a nonbeliever hearing it for the first time. Use language a person will understand. When I do this, I will not speak to them in a "preaching voice" but a more conversational one—as though I were speaking to them one-on-one.

I say something like, "You may have joined our service today as a visitor. Let me say first of all we are so glad you are here. We have been talking about (fill in the blank here for whatever your topic was). But you may not yet have this personal relationship with Jesus Christ. Let me break it down for you right now." Then I will share the gospel.

There are certain elements that must be in play for the gospel to be the gospel. We need to tell people they are separated from God by sin, that Jesus died for that sin, and that if they repent and turn to Him, they can be saved. Our message is "Christ and Him crucified."

Paul said, "I am not ashamed of the gospel of Christ, for it is the power of God to salvation" (Rom. 1:16). There is power in the simple message of the life, death, and resurrection of Jesus.

You need to start giving invitations for people to come to Christ. This takes a commitment, because there is always the possibility of failure. But there is an even greater possibility of success. It's worth the risk. At the end of your message should be an evangelistic "hook." No matter what the topic, there is always a way to wrap it up evangelistically. The key is to transition to the cross. Preach this part of your message with urgency, "as a dying man to dying men." You must trust that God will bless His Word and convict people of sin.

When Peter was preaching on the day of Pentecost, they were "cut to the heart," and they asked, "What shall we do?" (Acts

2:37). In verses 38–39, Peter replied, "Each of you must repent of your sins and turn to God, and be baptized in the name of Jesus Christ for the forgiveness of your sins. Then you will receive the gift of the Holy Spirit. This promise is to you, and to your children, and even to the Gentiles—all who have been called by the Lord our God" (NLT).

Like Peter, you must be intentional in your invitation, preaching for a decision.

3. Be Clear in Your Invitation

This is where it breaks down for most preachers. I have heard pastors and speakers give excellent messages with a call to Christ. Then it all falls apart in "the mechanics" of it. People do not understand what you are asking them to do.

By the way, there are many ways to go about calling someone to Christ. There are a lot of ways to ask people to respond to your invitation. You can have people stand up and pray, you can have them pray with you and then send them to a room for follow-up, you can have them come forward to the front and lead them in prayer. The main thing is that we call them to Christ. There needs to be a "moment of decision." We don't have the specifics of an invitation in Scripture, but we have many instances of people repenting and believing in large numbers.

4. Have a Follow-up System in Place

I'm talking about counselors who have been trained to encourage new believers. If a church does not have a follow-up ministry for new converts, something is not right. A church that does not have a constant flow of new believers will stagnate. New converts are the lifeblood of the church. We have a choice: evangelize or fossilize.

The early church—the church that changed the world— had a constant flow of new converts. Acts 2:46–47 tells us, "So continuing daily with one accord in the temple, and breaking bread from house to house, they ate their food with gladness and simplicity of heart, praising God and having favor with all the people. And the Lord added to the church daily those who were being saved."

5. Start and Maintain an Evangelistic Culture

People always return to mediocrity, so you must not let this culture die. A crusade or rally can help, but ongoing evangelism is something you must do in your church. Your people must invite others to church! In almost all cases, new converts at our crusades end up in the church of the person who brought them.

If you just announce an evangelistic outreach event and put out invitations, you might see some growth. But if you urge and exhort your people to bring nonbelievers, it will grow.

If you are thinking, *That just won't work in our church!* then change the culture of your church so it will. Do a series on the importance of sharing one's faith. My experience has taught me that the presentation of the gospel followed by an invitation to receive Christ can be effective in a multitude of environments and settings.

Let's all pray for an evangelistic culture in our churches.

About the Author

Greg Laurie is the senior pastor of Harvest Christian Fellowship in Riverside and Orange County in California. Harvest is one of the largest churches in the United States and consistently ranks among the most influential churches in the country. He recently celebrated forty years as the senior pastor. In 1990, he began holding large-scale public evangelistic events called Harvest Crusades. More than five million people have attended Harvest events around the world, and more than five hundred thousand people have registered professions of faith through these outreaches.

He is the featured speaker of the nationally syndicated radio program *A New Beginning*, which is broadcast on more than seven hundred radio outlets worldwide. Along with his work at Harvest Ministries, he served as the 2013 honorary chairman of the National Day of Prayer and also serves on the board of directors of the Billy Graham Evangelistic Association.

He has authored more than seventy books, including *As It Is in Heaven, Revelation: The Next Dimension, As I See It, Hope for Hurting Hearts, Married, Happily, Every Day with Jesus, Signs of the Times, Hope for America,* and his autobiography, *Lost Boy.*

He has been married to Cathe Laurie for forty-one years, and they have two sons, Christopher and Jonathan. Christopher went to be with the Lord in 2008. They also have five grandchildren.

Notes

1. C. S. Lewis, *Letters to Malcolm: Chiefly on Prayer* (San Diego: Harcourt, 1963), 91.

2. Charles H. Spurgeon, *Sermons Preached and Revised* (London: Passmore & Alabaster, 1877), 143–44.

3. Charles H. Spurgeon, *The Treasury of David* (London: Passmore & Alabaster, 1886), 15.

4. Billy Graham, http://www.billygraham.info/best-quotes-by-billy-graham/we-are-the-bibles-the-world-is-reading-billy-graham.

5. Charles Spurgeon, *The Metropolitan Tabernacle Pulpit*, Volume 7, "The Wailing of Risca," sermon delivered December 9, 1860.

6. Material taken from a George Barna Poll. Date unknown.

7. D. L. Moody quote taken from "Inspirational Quotes" compiled by Steve Shirley on jesusalive.cc/quotes.html.

8. Timothy Keller, *The Reason for God* (New York: Penguin Books, 2008), 67.

9. C. S. Lewis, *The Great Divorce* (New York: HarperCollins, 1946, 1973), 75.

10. Cathy Lynn Grossman, *USA TODAY*, http://www.usatoday.com/story/news/nation/2012/10/08/nones-protestant-religion-pew/1618445.

11. See http://www.pewforum.org/2012/10/09/nones-on-the-rise.

12. Malcom Muggeridge quote found on http://www.goodreads.com/quotes/726614-all-new-news-is-old-news-happening-to-new-people.

13. Chuck Swindoll, *Paul: A Man of Grace and Grit* (Nashville: W Publishing Group, 2002), 39.

14. Spurgeon, *Sermons Preached and Revised*, 143–44.